# 500MILES

## *"I would walk (500 miles)"*

*with thanks to
The Proclaimers who kindly
endorsed our endeavour.*

# 500MILES

## WALKING TOWARDS AN INDEPENDENT SCOTLAND

Dean Woodhouse
Jim Stewart
Laura Marshall
Nicholas Russell
Dave Llewellyn

1st Monochrome Edition - August 2020
ISBN: 9798680002131

The text in this book has been written based on personal experiences. All contributors have made all reasonable efforts to ensure that the details are correct at the time of publication. The authors cannot accept responsibility for any omissions, but would be happy to incorporate additions and corrections in future editions.

# IN MEMORY OF

*Margaret Pollock,*
*Jacqueline Watson and*
*Aidan McCormack.*
*Thank you for being part of our journey.*

## Desiderium

A longing or ardent desire as for something once
possessed and now missed; pain or regret
on account of loss or absence.

*from the century dictionary*

# FOREWORD

"What do we want?" A bed for the night.
"When do we want it?" As soon as you like.

The walkers and their back-up team, neither too wee
or stupid started their lang walk from Skye to Edinburgh
and in this lovely book the authors describe their
journey warts an' a'. Their traits, their strengths on view
but most of all their inner courage and commitment
which they had in spades.

The walkers' road across Scotland was not without
bumps, just like oor journey to Independence. But if
ever we lack confidence or inspiration we should just
read this book and oor resolve will be strengthened.

Their road was littered with YES support and not a
campaign in sight! Memorable pictures, some great
music, hospitality (not just Highland) and even some
original poetry, all remind the walkers of a time they'll
never forget and we owe them a lot for their selfless
act. They met some wonderful people, not all in favour
of Independence of course. But as is abundantly clear
in the book, a country's path to autonomy will only be

successful if we bring people along in a positive way, not by telling them they're stupid!

The authors describe well oor beautiful wee country but after a lifetime in active campaigning I would add that we're also a mongrel Nation, which is all the better for having so many people from a' the airts coming to bide here.

The book rightly mentions absent friends, some weelkent and some less so but all sorely missed. I would like to add a stalwart activist sadly taken from us earlier this month (August 2020) after a short, but very serious illness. "We've got yer back hen and will tak ye wi' us". Margaret (Magrit) Pollock was a retired School-Heidie and a dear freen who is depicted in the book when the walkers came to the Blether-In, Forfar (See her cake).

Now to the song which has been lent to us for the occasion:

"And when the money comes in for the work I do

I'll pass along every cent of it to you"

It's time we stopped passing oor money to Westminster only to be given some back as pocket money-Bye Bye, Barnett Formula, hello takin' care o' oor ain, makin' oor ain decisions.

The walkers knew where they came from, they knew where they were going. Wi' a fair win' at oor backs, we can a' join them on the "Road to Independence".

Linda Clark
August 23rd 2020

# CONTENTS

# HANDS OFF OUR PARLIAMENT
## FRIDAY MARCH 23TH 2018

TÚS MAITH, LEATH NA HOIBRE.

In the beginning of 2018, some of the prominent members of the Yes movement were starting to get itchy feet. It felt like nothing was happening to promote Scotland as an independent country, while at the same time Westminster was doing everything it could to belittle Scotland for objecting to Brexit.

With cross party support, the Scottish Government successfully passed the Continuity Bill which was Scotland's alternative to Westminster's EU Withdrawal Bill. The bill's passage caused ripples in the legal landscape, resulting in the bill going to court to determine it's legality.

Subsequent actions from Theresa May's government had made it appear as if they were on a course to dilute the devolved powers to the governments in Scotland and Wales (Northern Ireland's devolved government had already been dissolved).

The appearance of a power-grab resulted in a push to stand up and be seen. A group of organisers under the name "Hands Around Parliament", all of whom had already gained experience setting up independence marches across Scotland, made the decision to promote a symbolic and peaceful protest at Holyrood, calling it *Hands Off Our Parliament*. These included Cliff Serbie, TC Charlton, Agnes Thomson and Graham Jones. Dave Llewellyn was also involved as a troubleshooter and talked with the media and worked on Twitter and Facebook to get the word out.

The plan was to gather enough people to link hands around the public perimeter of the Scottish Parliament building at Holyrood on the morning on 23rd March - a day that wouldn't disrupt government business as the government typically does the majority of its work from Tuesday to Thursday). Unlike the previous independence marches, the organisers stressed this was a pro-devolution demonstration supporting the Continuity Bill that was backed by the *Scottish Greens*, *Scottish Labour*, *Liberal Democrats* as well as the *SNP*.

A good many turned up for the event, which included a rally on the green space beside Holyrood. Organisers handed out badges that had been made by George Page to attendees. The organisers had used the symbol of a black hand in front of a persons face surrounded by a red circle with a red line through it akin to a *do not enter* health and safety sign sometimes seen in Europe. *Hands Off Our Parliament #HOOP* was used alongside.

Hundreds of flags were waving in the breeze. Most were the blue and white St. Andrews Cross - the Saltire, some with Yes imprinted on them. A few Lion Rampant flags were flying too. Catalan flags were also present, showing their solidarity with Catalonia, who were also facing a similar situation trying to get their independence from Spain.

Banners were there in abundance, including

2

*#KeepScotlandTheBrand*, *Women for Independence*, *Pensioners for Independence*, *Common Weal*, the *SNP* and of course the event itself held by some of the organisers including Lyndsey Peebles. Independence activists Paul Kavanagh (also known as the *Wee Ginger Dug*) and Peter Bell were amongst a dozen speakers addressing the crowd before proceeding to link hands.

The event was a roaring success with estimates between 3000 and 5000 people attending, circling the entire public area around Holyrood, and in front of the building the people were between two and 5 people deep. The atmosphere was electric and uplifting, which was a godsend considering the downheartedness that had brought everyone there. It was nothing short of a demonstration, that residents of Scotland are determined to retain everything that had been won from Westminster.

Before the event finished, there was a presentation of shields - made from plywood in two sizes - a large one that was 3 feet tall and a smaller one half that size. With the exception of the large shield that Cliff Serbie held with a Lion Rampant, all the rest were painted with a St. Andrews Cross Saltire design. There were 100 shields distributed that day. Laura Marshall got her smaller sized shield, that she would carry everywhere, gathering signatures on the back from independence supporters along her travels The signature she was most proud of, in the heart of the shield, would shortly come from Nicola Sturgeon herself.

# THE GATHERING

### TRÍ NA CHÉILE A THÓGTAR NA CÁISLÉAIN.

The Brexit process (or lack thereof) was starting to make people re-assess the implications for Scotland's future. How could Scotland break free now? Hope was in short supply. But some members of the Yes movement were determined to keep the fire burning and be ready at a moment's notice.

In November 2013 the Scottish Government, lead by the SNP, published a white paper to outline how Scotland could be governed following a Yes vote in the "2014 Scottish referendum for independence from the United Kingdom". In retrospect, this document became what many thought to be a tombstone that created more questions than answers. The UK focused media had a field day picking it apart. Whether or not it was meant only as a blueprint was irrelevant. The end result was that many potential Yes voters would get cold feet. Arguably, the SNP hadn't the public relations 'bandwidth' or a sympathetic media outlet to counter the attacks in time. The Daily Record's printing of "The Vow" was all that was needed to make the 'mebbies' turn to No.

Brexit was described by a leaflet that was distributed south of the border as "The Truth" and was anything but. It was heavy on promises about £350million a week being sent to the NHS instead of Europe (mentioned 3 times), control of immigration (which we already had, but the Home Office chose not to enforce) and more empty promises that were quickly brushed under the carpet. In a surprise to all it worked, helped by a mainstream media that intentionally didn't question anything about it. Only later would we begin to discover how external forces (Cambridge Analytica and Facebook) plus the work of the Tory-funded media would ultimately make the Orwellian IngSoc mindthink appear to become fully realised. Regardless of how everyone voted, we all lost to government control.

In both cases, the right-wing mindset was made with the convenient retort - that this was a referendum to end all referendums. Yet nothing that was promised from the winning side of either referendum was actually realised. All talk of promises of devo-max or devo-light was replaced with *English Votes for English Laws* (or *EVEL*), which locked out MP's from Scotland on legislation that didn't directly affect them.

A prime example of how this lack of input to EVEL legislation could harm Scotland involves the NHS. Although *NHS Scotland* is managed by the Scottish Government, its budget is linked to the budget of the NHS in England; the budget for the Scottish NHS is approximately 10% of the budget for England, and if English MP's vote to privatise more and reduce the money allocated to the actual NHS infrastructure, then NHS Scotland loses an equal proportion of its budget, whilst Scottish MP's are denied any say in the matter.

So much for the supposed "Union of equals".

During a live debate two weeks before the Scottish independence referendum in September 2014, Ruth Davidson MSP said on Scottish Television that a vote for "no means we stay in, we're members of the European Union". In hindsight this seemed an odd statement to make, when the Tories pledged to allow a Brexit referendum vote at the Conservative Party Conference held in Birmingham just eleven days after Scotland had voted. Ruth was one of the main speakers at that conference, speaking as the leader of the Scottish Conservatives at that time. She was left with no choice than to change her stance on Brexit and back the main party.

Scotland can undoubtedly state that after voting against a split from Europe (with a "remain" majority in every single constituency), it was on solid ground trying to argue for a better Brexit deal than the breadcrumbs Westminster was offering. The media couldn't stop this argument, though it did the best it could to prevent Scotland having a voice, by shutting out any representation.

David Mundell MP, the then Secretary of State for Scotland, promised to work in Scotland's interests by bringing amendments that would protect Scotland's devolved powers. He then neglected to introduce any amendments before the six month deadline. The only thing Mundell had accomplished during his time as Secretary of State was to build a high security Scottish Office building next to Waverley Station that would house 3000 workers, even though few could fathom why Mundell would need something so big and hire so many.

While the Brexit process was "on going", more and more of the promises from "the vow" were turning into unfulfilled lies. The SNP led Scottish Government was propping up the Scottish NHS, while the English NHS south of the border was being reported by the media as having one meltdown after another. The British media controlled the narrative by persistently mentioning the NHS, when it always meant the *English NHS*, trying to tar NHS Scotland with the very same brush. Stories started leaking of how some hospital procedures in England were no longer being offered for free. Privatisation by the back door was being realised. Readers interested in discovering more should search for the John Pilger film "The Dirty War on the NHS".

The EU migrants were having to deal with one threat after another, and many lost patience with the limbo of uncertainty and packed their bags. Scotland was the only part of the UK that offered local EU migrants help, recognising that they were a valuable asset to Scotland. But the Scottish Government's hands were largely tied because matters regarding immigration are not devolved. Attempts to cover the costs of EU residency paperwork by the Scottish Government were quickly shot down by the then prime minister, Theresa May.

Thanks to Brexit, the media has inadvertently given Scotland a perfect storm, identifying everything that is wrong with Westminster and its relationship with the rest of the UK and Europe. For Scots who didn't subscribe to the Westminster controlled media outlets, the writing was already on the wall. Many of those that remained have slowly shifted away from the half truths that have been keeping them from realising the full extent of the bias and lies made to keep Westminster in power. Democracy in Westminster had failed and the Conservatives repeatedly made poor decisions that make that realisation more and more obvious. Scotland has remembered Europe as the hand that helped when Thatcher and New Labour gave it the short straw.

After 18 months of what seemed like UK Government anarchy trying to wrestle Brexit into something that reflected what leave voters intended, a number of members of the Yes movement tried to get the 'party back together' and get some momentum towards escaping Brexit, showing our strength and walking our own path.

The Gathering #1 (hosted on 24th May, 2018) was organised by the National Yes Registry, who had also been involved with building the IndyApp (which tells anyone who installs it, where to find their local Yes group and any planned events). The data from the IndyApp made them a good fit for organising a get-together to discuss how to move forward. Members from the various Yes groups were invited to get together to discuss strategies and issues surrounding the independence movement. On the day, twenty two tables were designated with a topic, and up to sixteen people were allowed to sign up for each table.

Dean Woodhouse was there early and chose to sit at table three discussing the most signed up for topic: Currency. Laura Marshall was also there on table six discussing the issue of what to do with the nuclear weapons. Dave Llewellyn was present, holding a banner and watching over the first half of the discussions from the floor above. All the attendees were given a vote to decide what topics to discuss in more detail for round two. Dean left early to get his photographs and copy published in *The National* the following day.

After winning one of the topics for further discussion, table twenty one continued to discuss the idea for 'the big bang' - i.e. what one thing could be done to bring attention to the Yes movement. At that table, sat Dave Llewellyn, *IndyPoet* Paul J Colvin, Paul Wright and Laura Marshall amongst numerous others. Ideas were thrown around but the overwhelming concept was to follow in the footsteps of the famous song "I would walk (500 miles)" by independence supporters, *The Proclaimers*. The table assembled a slide show (like all other tables) outlining a suggestion for an "I would walk 500 miles" event.

Dave had been involved with helping to organise and steward a number of recent independence events and decided to take up the process of organising the 500 miles event.

After the Gathering was done, the primary discussion topics had been helpful to determine just what mattered to Scotland and this lead to a second Gathering later. While everyone discussed topics that were invaluable to understanding what we wanted to take forward in Scotland, the 500 miles event would become the one thing that was actually acted upon afterwards.

Later in July, Dave sent out a request for volunteers to walk all 500 miles. The call for walkers was extended to anyone involved with the Yes movement. Expectedly, responses came in slowly due to the logistics of being away for three weeks. Others would require getting a check-up and an okay at their doctors for covering any potential health concerns.

Each walker had their own personal reasons for why

they were going to do the walk. That was understood from the outset.

In an online video post of his, Nicholas summed up the point of the walk as follows: "#500miles celebrates the right of Scotland's people to self-determination, civil rights, equality, fairness, and inclusion".

Laura carried her HOOP Shield (one of the 100 shields made by Cliff Serbie, TC Charlton, Faye from Fife and Agnes Thompson who made Laura's shield) throughout the walk, collecting thousands of signatures and photographs of people who had held it. These had already included Nicola Sturgeon and Clara Ponsatí, plus many names from the wider Yes movement.

Dean decided to walk to show that there was nothing that Scotland could not accomplish, and had every intention of getting the team to Edinburgh. As a professional photographer, realising the importance of the walk, he also wanted to record the events along the way and eventually document this little piece of history.

Many also walked for promoting *Blockchain Democracy* (described in detail later in the book), the new *Scottish Covenant Association* and Pat Lee's *Doorstep Referendum*, the last two were involved with collecting signatures to make the case for Scottish independence. We all walked thanks to some help from *Saor Alba*, who were behind the high-level organisation with the logistics.

We all marched to promote hope of a free and independent Scotland while connecting the many Yes communities scattered across the country.

# MEET YOU IN SKYE

## FÉASTA ANOCHT AGUS GORTA AMÁRACH.

It may come as a surprise, but the 500 mile walkers really hadn't actually met or talked to each other before meeting up on the way to Skye. There were numerous suggestions about a meeting to figure out logistics and such, but that never came to be.

The 500 mile walkers came from various parts of the country and had very different backgrounds. Dave had hoped for ten walkers to come forward, and a few pulled out shortly beforehand. One was a legitimate health concern, another was due to family commitments. Ultimately it didn't matter, so long as the team made it to the end. The walkers were Dave Llewellyn, Jim Stewart, Wren Chapman, Karl J Claridge, Nicholas Russell, Dean Woodhouse and Laura Marshall. They came from Edinburgh, Glasgow, Kirriemuir, Markinch, Strathaven and West Linton. They came from very different backgrounds and three of them were born in England - much to the surprise of many who later tried to accuse the 500 mile walkers of hating the English.

It was September 14th 2018 when we all drove up to the Isle of Skye to meet at the camp site at Sligachan.

Our arrangements on Skye had been setup by Carole Inglis of *Yes Skye & Lochalsh* who put Dave in contact with Sandy Coghill who owns the campsite at Sligachan.

Prior to this the main convoy met up at Edinburgh, and then met up with two other walkers who had carpooled and met at Spean Bridge. Two-toned hi-visibility vests were handed out, which became our stand out identification - the blue lower half said Walker on the back.

It was unfortunate that we hadn't met up before the camp site as we had lots to talk about. We all ate at the restaurant across the street from the camp site where we also met up with local independence celebrity Steve and his two famous dogs *Blaze* and *Laoch*.

Many of us stayed up late that night and unfortunately the sound of heated discussions travels easily through tent fabrics and nearby campers. Not surprisingly those of us in the tent received a bit of a telling off for being noisy by two campers. We felt bad, but the end of their comment took us by surprise: "it doesn't help your cause".

We had Saltires and Yes flags flying around our group camp. The following day, our presence was already on social media and the pro-union supporting campers had taken to publishing photographs of us and somehow noticed that a number of vehicles in the camp site were recently untaxed. One of the drivers' cars was one of them, which turned out to be an unexpected delay (from the DVLA processing the payment and the subsequent online update). It was then we knew that the pro-union social media were going to play dirty.

The start of the walk was supposed to begin at Portree, but a local funeral put an end to that plan. So the official start would be at the bridge at Sligachan.

An hour before the start, stalls had been setup beside the nearby restaurant. There was a stall selling merchandise promoting the 500 miles walk that had been generously put together by George Page & Cath Rolland from *Lomond Graphics & Promotions*. Carole Inglis and Hector Macleod from Yes Skye & Lochalsh had a stall, as did the local SNP branch. We'd like to thank Carole Inglis and Hector Macleod for all their help setting everything up here on Skye.

It should be mentioned at this point that the 500 miles walk was not crowd-funded. It wasn't operating as a charity and we had no money to speak of at the beginning. It was hoped that charity in the form of donations and board & lodging would be all that was needed. The crowd-funding idea was put to bed because there had been so many of them for various independence causes that year, and the organisers thought it would be too much to ask again. So the alternative idea was to create a means to sell merchandise, which would in turn fund the walk. There was supposed to be an online shop to sell the merchandise, but somehow this didn't happen. We would later discover this was due to the payment company having issues, due to how the account was setup and it was never resolved. The merchandise was ordered and available at spots along the walk. Due to this oversight, finances for food expenses were down to the walkers themselves until after the first day was over.

On a positive note, The Proclaimers' manager Kenny MacDonald endorsed the event wishing us "the very best with your endeavours around the I would walk 500 miles march". They might have actually joined in for a while were it not for the fact they were on tour in America.

A number of articles had already been published in The National newspaper bringing to attention the event and the desire to join up Yes groups across the country and get people to walk along side and do their part.

After a summer of record breaking hot weather, it was no surprise that the tide had turned back to "normal". The normal weather on Skye is always changeable. Overnight camping in Sligachan was damp with dry spells. Many of the walkers had to pack up their damp tents and load them into one of three different support vehicles before getting ready for the start of the walk at midday.

Laura had brought her shield, and had photographs taken with numerous people. On the back, many people had already signed it. So she made sure that Ian Blackford MP also added his signature. Laura was to carry this shield everywhere she walked.

At noon, the party and a crowd of forty or so started walking from the restaurant towards the bridge. Lead by a piper, drummer and a couple of Yes Bikers members. At the middle of the bridge, Ian Blackford MP stood and gave his passionate speech while the two 'Indy dugs', Laoch and Blaze sat politely next to him with their owner Steve on the wall of the bridge. Ian said:

"Here today, it's probably worth reminding people that in the referendum campaign we had way back in 2014 there were a number of us active in that campaign.

"We fought a momentous campaign here on Skye. We went to every township that we could. We had 70 public meetings over the course of the two year campaign for us. There was a real excitement, there was a real pas-

sion, and I think for the people of Skye could see that
we had a vision for a new Scotland. That passion that
we put across to the people of Skye was rewarded.

"On the referendum day we were of course devastat-
ed by the result from some of the parts of Scotland. But
I can tell you that Skye is a Yes island. We won the vote.
Skye voted 54% to take back our freedom and inde-
pendence, so we can build that new, fairer, prosperous
Scotland that we all wish for.

"The 500 mile march is something, as I said, that's
iconic. What was it? Taken from the words of the Proclaimers Song. I know, I believe, that we will win back
our freedom, we will win our independence. It will
happen. Scotland will become a nation represented in
the United Nations, and what you are doing with this
walk is so important. And I hope what it does do, is that
it inspires people.

"That we have a conversation with the people of Scotland. That we know that, I know that, many people want
us to have the referendum tomorrow, there will be a
referendum on Scotland's future. The Scottish National
Party has a mandate for a referendum on Scotland's
future, and we won that on the election in 2016.

"What the First Minister has said is we will make sure
that we know the destination for Brexit and we will have
that conversation. We know we need to protect the people of Scotland from what is happening here, as to what
a hard Brexit would do to the people of Scotland.

"We know there's a threat to prosperity; We know
there's a threat to jobs, and it's up to us to provide that
leadership. To have that conversation with the people
of Scotland. To take them by the hand and ask them to
complete the journey that began when Scotland voted
for devolution in 1997. That they trust us, that they trust
ourselves, that we can deliver that society that we all

want to see.

"And when we put all that in the context of where you are here, in Skye, one of the other reasons I'm so pleased, so proud that you're here today, when you talk about the movement for land reform, people's rights, it began here in Skye.

"So lets start a march today for Scotland's freedom, starting right here on Skye. Taking us to Edinburgh and we wish you all the success in that march."

Ian Blackford then rang the Freedom Bell that had been provided by Mike Fenwick, before shaking hands with Dave Llewellyn and handing him the bell to carry on along the march.

Dave then said "I have a dream, let freedom ring" before ringing the bell. This was then repeated by Laura, Wren, Lyndsey, Pat. Nicholas then said "I have a dream, I want to see Blockchain Democracy for all Scotland" before ringing the bell to cheer from the crowd. Jim then took on the original call and rang the bell, then Karl, Dean and finally our driver John Robertson who said "I have a dream, freedom will ring".

After Ian had finished his speech, the group gathered behind him on the bridge while he cut the tape of satires to mark the start of the walk. Ian Blackford said "Okay then, well good luck" to lots of thank you's.

# CROSSING SKYE
## SATURDAY SEPTEMBER 15TH

### BÍONN GACH TOSÚ LAG.

The walkers walked behind the lead car driven by John Robertson, who had decorated it with a number of flags both large and small, stickers and flashing hazard lights. The front of the car had a bonnet cover with a Saltire and the words "Yes We Can" in plain sight.

The wind had picked up, enough to keep most flags flying horizontally without any problem. The mist was thick on the hills beside and behind us and fortunately much clearer and dry in front. Nicholas had brought a special flag and flagpole. The "Blockchain Saltire" flag was designed by "Brave" (Twitter: @defiaye) and contained thousands of small profile photos from Twitter followers for YesDayScotland, assembled to resemble a Saltire. Nicholas had taken the image and had it printed on a flag.

As we began to walk along the road, we were visited by a local Lochaber and Skye police officer who drove in front of us before pulling over and walking with us. PC Andrew Sykes was there to brief us on how we were to walk (in close groups), what to do when irate drivers caused issues (just give way for our own safety), and what our rights were (we were fully entitled to walk in single file, or in a group behind a lead car on any highway except a controlled highway such as a motorway). We had to wear our hi-visibility vests at all times and any additional walkers we encountered were recommended to do the same.

At first the discussion was somewhat tense, but seemingly PC Sykes understood we were happy to listen, heed his advice and appreciated his efforts. After walking with us for a half mile, he departed and we set on our way. At this point the weather was relatively dry with a few dreary spells and mist in the distance - nothing we weren't expecting on Skye.

A number of extra walkers stayed with us the entire first day including Pat Lee, Lyndsey Peebles and David Cox. Pat is a good friend of Dave Llewellyn and wanted to walk with us as long as he could. Lyndsey had originally planned on walking for the first weekend but would end up walking with us for much longer. Lyndsey was an invaluable asset to the group, as she helped Dave with organisation. David Cox from Yes Nairn, was an experienced hiker, and joined us for the first and last day of our walk (and subsequently wrote about his No-to-Yes experience in *The National* a month later). David offered his walking sticks to Laura, after observing that she had twisted her ankle prior to the walk, hoping that they would help relieve the pain.

Margaret McVicar and Barbara Martin, members of the local Yes Skye & Lochalsh group, joined us for the first few miles, leaving us at the ferry terminal at Sconser (where they would travel on to Rathsay). After thanking them for joining us for the start of our hike, we trudged on.

We walked along the left side of road in rows of two, with the car behind us. And for the most part, it was a rather uneventful time where we talked and finally got to know each other. Since we were taking up an entire lane and walking just 3 miles per hour, we were obviously holding up traffic. But with the help of our driver and the walker in front, we waved them past and many of them gave us a positive response. Waves, horns honking and the occasional photograph with a mobile phone and a cheer. Some people also threw change out their window for us to pickup as they passed by, which was appreciated.

After a while, and to make the walk more eventful, Pat made this amusing by trying to predict which way the drivers swayed - shouting "good guy" for Yes supporters based on the driver feedback. We did find that it seemed like 95% of cars tooting on Skye were "good guys".

We should mention that the process of how we reacted with the members of the public we met was a bit of an evolutionary process after we came across a number of rather hostile responses from people on Skye. Since word got out about the walk, some locals who were obviously shaken by our event felt the need to hurl verbal abuse at us. We never once responded as if we were offended, but instead waved and smiled whenever we met someone. The process of getting folk from No to Yes required that we be on our best behaviour and keep a positive attitude. We had 500 miles to go, and show we could do whatever we put our minds to.

We used the lay-by to let the tailbacks pass, but when we approached Blackhill, we hit our first problem. The car had a manual gearbox and our driver John was having to ride the clutch and use the brakes to try to keep a safe distance behind us. After the past few miles of slow hill driving, it was starting to smell hot. We briefly pulled over into a lay-by and putting on our best mechanic's hat, determined the brakes and coolant were both normal. The clutch was probably the culprit and we couldn't do anything about it at that point.

At the car park near the Blackhill waterfall, Dave saw a camper van that looked a lot like the one at the various marches for selling burgers and stovies. So we got our hopes up that he had coordinated this, only to find that it wasn't the same van. There were no such plans and now we felt hungry. We let the car have a brief cooling down break and then plodded on past the Blackhill Waterfall, alongside Loch Ainort and into the village of Luib where the weather started to turn.

We were hoping that Luib had somewhere to have a sit down and a cup of tea, but we found nothing obvious and plodded on. The two women of our group were getting uncomfortable and needed a toilet break, but there was nowhere to go. Fortunately at the next lay-by alongside the A87, we met up again with the couple with their camper van who were members of Yes Skye & Lochalsh and graciously offered the women the use of their toilet.

We quickly realised this was something that would be needed more often, especially as we crossed over the highlands. The organisers had brought a little bit of food, but the planning was really not well thought through - not unexpected when nobody had done or planned a multi-day event before. Dave shared out bars of a donated box of tablet from Skye, which gave us a needed boost as we plodded on.

About a mile outside Broadford we had to stop. Dave was starting to have trouble walking - limping along like his feet were on fire. It was starting to drizzle with rain, and Dave had walked over 15 miles with old shoes and no socks. We took a break in a lay-by and demanded that Dave sit in the car with John before the rest of the walkers continued into Broadford. The rain gained intensity as we walked.

The intentions for the day were to walk as far as Kyleakin which would have been just shy of 25 miles, but there was now a problem with this plan - the sun was going down and our presence on a busy road did not help things when it was pouring down with rain and conditions were getting worse. We were all drenched and stopped under the awning at the Cafe Sia to try to decide what to do while enjoying hot drinks from the shop. Time was fast running out and realistically we couldn't continue walking in dangerous conditions. So we had to figure out how to handle the fact that the vehicles needed to shuttle us and our gear were in different locations.

John took Dave and Nicholas back to Sligachan to return to their cars, while the rest of us were wondering what the plans were for the night. We would soon discover that we were expected to camp in Kyleakin.

Dean, Laura, Karl and Wren were first to be picked up by Dave and were to be taken to Kyleakin only to discover that the entire camp site (and everything else in town) was full of bikers visiting Skye for their annual Shoot the Goose Rally weekend.

Discovering this, everything started to go haywire. It was obvious there was no alternative plan for somewhere to stay and panic set in. Nicholas, who had his own car (and wasn't aware of the plans anyway) drove to the opposite side of the bridge and found a place to spend the night in Kyle of Lochalsh. The rest of us tried to see what we could do in Kyleakin.

We were split up into groups as we had to be ferried around in one car (John's car was loaded with our gear). The first four of us to be ferried to Kyleakin were dropped off at the Saucy Mary's Lodge and sat down in the pub. We didn't get there until after 9pm and the kitchen had closed for the night. We were already getting low on energy and cash (and Wren had lost her bank card). Choices were sparse, so pizza and chips it was. We got a pitcher of water to quench our thirst.

Laura had joked, "give me 30 minutes and I'll talk my magic to try to get somewhere to stay", walking off to the bar for another pitcher.

Laura offered the barman some money to setup a mattress in the pub, and he said "Had it been a hotel room and not a bar he would have, but you'd drink me dry!" The bikers, all joking, said "Give her a break".

The hotel boss from the King George Hotel next door just happened to walk in, and the barman insisted he try to give Laura a room. Noticing Laura's walking vest and Yes badges, remembered there was a room reserved for another Yes supporter who wouldn't arrive until the wee hours. He showed Laura a picture of the person on his phone asking if she recognised them. Laura said he looked familiar, so he called the hotel to make arrangements.

Not knowing what Laura had accomplished, the other 500 mile walkers in the pub thought it was looking like a lost cause. We had no idea where we were expected to sleep, what to eat, who was going to fund and plan. Mentally and physically exhausted, many of us were not in a good place, waiting for the rest of the team to show up.

After a while, Dean disappeared to try to find the rest of the team, discovering Dave, Lyndsey and John were sitting in their cars escaping the pouring rain. Laura found Karl and Wren waiting for her.

The biker's were everywhere, which had made it difficult for the other team members to find those sitting in the pub. This meant that they stayed outside waiting and in a moment of desperation Jim and Pat had set up their tents on the grass. Had any of us actually scoped out Kyleakin beforehand, we would have setup somewhere less exposed, because that night was the beginning of Storm Aileen blowing in from the west.

We discovered that John, our driver and first aider, had serious issues with constant back pain, which made him a somewhat tetchy. An army veteran, he was not happy about the poor planning and felt bad for us. He repeated that he was taught never to leave anyone behind.

Tension between John and the other organisers was starting to mount. He'd been quite demanding about how we stayed in line on the road. Some of the walkers showed concern about the amount of pain medication John was taking to do this task. But John had a heart of gold, and wanted to stick to it.

Laura and Wren went to their beds that Laura had arranged in the local hotel, while Dave, Lyndsey and John slept in the two cars. Dean, Jim and Pat camped on the grass lawn outside. There was an additional tent which we presumed was Karl's.

Those of us who camped out were not too happy with the arrangements. The location was perfect for hearing the roar of every single gust of wind about five seconds before the tent actually moved from the blast. To add another problem, the pub was having a late night party with the bikers, which didn't stop until after midnight. The other pub down the street was doing the same. The constant wind gave for temporary solace, but the gusts were getting stronger as the night wore on and wouldn't let up until the sun started to rise.

After a few hours of tossing and turning, Dean's tent was actually starting to leak - somewhat surprising since it was a '4-season' tent meant to handle anything! After finally falling to sleep, drips started to fall directly above his head, waking him up. He then discovered that in the haste of setting up the tent in the pouring rain, he'd not setup the tent correctly and part of the cover was starting to come undone.

Jim's tent was also getting a battering from the gusts of wind that hit a few seconds after hearing the wind's noise in the distance. He also couldn't sleep for the storm's roar and the heavy rain that accompanied it.

Both Dean and Jim felt it was beyond hope to try to sleep and instead resorted to checking their phones. After the chaotic and soggy first evening, seeing some of the unionists' negative comments on social media was really unwelcome. But in hindsight, there was an upside - we were all over Scottish Twitter and Facebook. Obviously we had successfully made an impact.

It was obvious that better planning had to happen and food supplies needed to be bought to get us through the Highlands and beyond. Without it, finishing would be unrealistic. And we had no choice - we had to finish what we'd started.

When we arrived on Skye, we had been told the organisers of the All Under One Banner march were predicting a turnout of 30,000 people in Edinburgh. One of our tasks would be to help make that number much, much larger.

# TO ACHNASHEEN
## SUNDAY SEPTEMBER 16TH

IS FEARR AN TSLÁINTE NÁ NA TÁINTE.

The first sight of dawn was a new beginning. After all the hassle of the previous night and the storm from hell passing overhead, it started to feel like hope was beginning to take over. The walkers who had found a hotel room for the night were out of contact with the rest of the team, so didn't know about the day's plan.

Fortunately there was a solid plan and over five dozen local Yes Skye & Lochalsh members were expected to gather on the lawn where we had camped last night to ring the "freedom bell" and walk us over the Skye bridge to meet on the other side for a sending off.

The campers amongst us had risen to windy but now relatively dry sky. Fortunately it was dry enough to put our tents away. It was then we discovered that the last remaining tent was empty (we'd assumed Karl was in it, but he'd somehow slept in a hotel room too).

The daylight revealed that we'd camped in full view of the loch - which explained why the gusts of wind had been relentless and brutal. Seeing this, we were surprised all our tents were still accounted for.

Dave, Dean, Pat and Jim walked across the street

to the gift shop at the Cafe Moil (Dave knew they were Yes supporters) for a wonderful cup of coffee and a roll. Throughout our walk, small gestures like this were welcome donations.

Shortly afterwards, over the local Yes supporters gathered on the green and Pat and Dave made speeches, offering the bell for everyone to ring and say a little word about independence. Mike's freedom bell was a large and clunky old thing - full of character and a fitting way of getting people to share their hopes with the world.

At 10am we set off towards the famous Skye bridge. Passing the remaining bikers putting their camping gear away, we got quite a few cheers. At this point the walkers who had enjoyed the comfort of a bed in the Kings Arms Hotel had joined us and the leaders of the march waited at the top of the hill for everyone both fast-and-slow to catch up. It had grown organically into quite a crowd.

We all walked, Saltires flying, across the Skye bridge to horns honking to cheer us all on. Skye had been friendly to us. From the front, it looked so wonderful to see so many locals participating in our event, and we all chatted to a large number of them as we crossed the bridge. Laura and Pat dropped to the back of the crowd and caught the names of walkers including Lori, Eliza, Janet McClune, Jim Soutar and Aunty Heather with her wee girl (who was holding "Gemma", her unicorn) all of whom had been getting ready for weeks to join the 500 miles walk. Most of us had no idea.

Crossing the road before getting into Kyle of Lochalsh, we stopped in a car park where the Yes Skye & Lochalsh members had setup a stall, offering us fruit and snacks for our journey onwards. They had a four feet tall Yes sign propped up at the side of the road, and many of the local Yes supporters asked for photographs with the walkers in front of their sign.

Mick Methven walked up to Laura and tapped her on the shoulder, asking for a shield photo. He had known the 500 miles were coming to Skye for weeks and had toyed with the idea of joining it. But he had felt so let down on the week of the 2014 IndyRef and everything that followed, that he didn't know if he really wanted to join us. His wife Evey had kicked him out the house that morning and told him to go meet us at the bridge. He felt like he was on a cloud after walking with the whole group over the Skye Bridge, and wanted to walk with us along the road to his house. He could see Laura's feet were sore from the previous day, so after a shield photograph he said his wife could treat our feet. He wanted to help us out because participating in the 500 miles walk had helped him find hope. We would quickly discover he wasn't alone.

We continued chatting for twenty minutes or so before moving on to the Co-op in town. Here Dave and Lyndsey picked up supplies for the day ahead, and in an unexpected act of kindness the Co-op managers offered us all a free cup of coffee. We also received a wonderful donation for our cause from the store manager. In the car park, we talked with a number of locals, all quite happy to talk about a future in an independent Scotland.

The next section was one of the most scenic sections of the walk as we proceeded to walk along the footpath through the Kyle of Lochalsh, Balmacara to Auchtertyre. An unbroken stretch of footpath along a busy road in the sunshine was an unexpected surprise. We were thankful to be joined by Mick who was a local tour guide and resident in Auchtertyre.

Just before we took a break, both Laura and Wren notice three white horses in a field opposite the path. Laura said it was a great sign as they looked a lot like unicorns.

Once we reached Mick's house, the Tarracliffe B&B, his wife Evey had prepared a wonderful home made soup and rolls for us. Bruce, their dog, was really friendly and made some of us realise we were already missing the company of our own pets back home.

Evey was an expert at foot care and after we had conceded that we needed help, she graciously patched up our already sore and tired feet. Many of us were starting to realise how important it was to take care of our health. Those of us that had slept rough the previous night were offered a shower, which was a relief since we were told we would be camping again that night. Mick cut up some of his boot liners to repair Laura's boots.

Nicholas had a memorable conversation with Evey, who was tending to Dave's feet at the time. Nicholas thought she said, "If Dave doesn't get significant medical attention for his feet, he won't make it to the A3"

Nicholas asked, "The A3, how far away is that?"

She replied, "No, not the A3, Day 3!"

Mick and Evey told us that they could not recommend the first part of the road to Achnasheen as it is a winding track with lots of blind spots - much too dangerous to walk on. As they were also tour guides for Skye (skye-tours.co.uk), they had transport that could ferry us all to a safe point to restart our trek. Dave had told us that the walk across the Highlands wouldn't be unbroken, so we presumed the miles would still be the same as our target.

Before leaving the house and having a final photograph with the shield, Mick said "that reminds me" and disappeared for a moment to drill four holes in to Laura's HOOP shield, adding cord which would make it much more convenient for her to carry it for the remainder of the walk.

At this point Pat left us to return home with a lift from Nicholas. The rest of us all boarded the SkyTours minibus and were driven to a quiet spot just shy of Coulags on the A890 where we resumed our hike. John drove his car behind the minibus.

On arrival, we were a little taken aback. This 'A' road started out as a single track road with passing places! Fortunately the traffic levels were also pleasantly quiet. The first few miles went through land that was either predominantly lined with damp pine trees or flanked by open landscapes following alongside Loch Dughaill for a while. The scenery was beautiful and the trees gave us a little shelter from the rain showers that blew through occasionally.

It was here that Dean noticed the large amount of litter strewn along the sides of the road. Oddly it was consistently about two pieces of litter, usually cans and plastic bottles, every METER (this didn't seem to let up for the entire walk to Aberdeen, where it oddly started to get to be less persistent). We were walking for Scotland and the sight of this neglect in such a remote point in the Highlands was really unpleasant.

While passing through Balnacara, we came across a house strewn with Union flags and realised just how out of place it looked. Located alongside a railway line, we wondered if it was meant to provoke a reaction from Scottish visitors on the train line to Kyle of Lochalsh - the end of the line for visitors to the area and onwards to Skye. We smirked and continued without making a fuss.

Shortly afterwards, Lyndsey got a lift from Dave to go ahead and help him set up our tents at the destination before sundown.

The road then sharply curved around under a railway bridge and magically became a normal two lane 'A' road - it looked like a major highway, minus the expected traffic! Oddly the landscape just seemed to open up. We could see for miles ahead, which didn't much help when you knew that you had to walk to that distant point. We passed the one and only building along this deserted stretch and saw that the daylight was already starting to fade.

Our driver John had held his distance behind us and in an effort to save his clutch, brakes and shins, had taken the tactic of letting us walk ahead. But now the darkness was creeping in, he was using his headlights to help illuminate our path. Fortunate, as none of us had the foresight to wear our torches. Some of us figured finding them would be a lottery anyway, based on what car our gear was in. In what appeared to be a cruel illusion, it looked like we could see the last bend in the distance before Achnasheen, only to find we were walking on a seemingly endless bend that lasted nearly two hours.

At around 9pm, the sun had completely set and we had finally made it to the roundabout at Achnasheen. In a mark of sheer relief, Karl ran around the deserted roundabout twice, making our driver look on in disbelief at how he still had any energy left. The rest of us were so tired that we didn't have the capacity to question it.

The walkers wondered where we were camping for the night but fortunately John knew exactly where to go. Apparently our plan was to park and camp on the lawn in the car park alongside Achnasheen train station. The station had an open toilet building, and enough grass to pitch our four tents and the next train wasn't due until the morning anyway. We were glad that Dave and Lyndsey had driven ahead and set up our tents because were didn't have the energy left to do it. We simply moved our personal belongings from the cars to our tents.

For the record, the walkers covered exactly 25 miles that day. We had a disagreement with the miles recorded on the first day, so Dean installed and used an application on his phone to track distance covered using GPS.

Earlier, Dean had shared his location on his mobile phone with his wife who was occasionally sharing it via Twitter. Dave said that had to stop, as the opposition supporters were starting to use it to pinpoint our location as we went on. So our exact location and route were never shared again after that point. Dave announced our start and approximate end points from that day onwards. We'd later discover that decision was to become both a blessing and a curse.

Exhausted and glad it was going to be a quiet night, we ignored the blanket of midges, washed up, climbed into our tents and quickly passed out. John parked and tried to sleep in his car, while Dave and Lyndsey slept in the front seats of Dave's car. Laura had discovered the clean toilets were warm and dry, and with the aid of a candle, she was able to work and sleep there.

It wasn't long before light rain started to fall.

Dave Llewellyn had approached Nicholas Russell, Scotland's Blockchain Democracy originator (via the YesDayScotland media portal in mid 2018) asking if the 500 miles walk could be used to promote Scotland's emerging Blockchain Democracy capabilities. In turn, Nicholas had offered to personally participate on the entire walk and deliver accurate media coverage.

This would require dry charging capabilities each night for laptop, iPad, smart phone and more. It was agreed that if Nicholas was to walk every day, then a support driver would need to regularly take him back to collect his 'mobile charging station', aka his car.

We would soon loose our primary support driver in Culloden which meant that this 'plan' quickly went straight out the window. From that point on Nicholas was required to return home in central Scotland each night, re-charging equipment and returning to meet the team the following morning. This added 2500 miles of driving to Nicholas' 500 miles of walking.

Similarly, to maximise our chances of success, Laura Marshall used her planning skills with requests for assistance with sustenance and accommodation, media updates, as well as maintaining records of all incoming financial donations and expenses.

Since the 500 miles walkers had never had a single meeting together about any of these arrangements, it required that they were delivered by the compelling desire for everyone simply to do what they could each do best for the team. Our collective objective was to get at least one walker over the finish line, and to do so in a way that would deliver positive media coverage that would get the word out.

The fact that five of the walkers would complete the full distance, speaks for itself. We all did what each of us had to do. It is even more remarkable to consider what was achieved by walking, considering the injuries all the walkers sustained.

# ONWARDS TO CULLODEN
## MONDAY SEPTEMBER 17TH

### BEIDH LÁ EILE AG AN BPAORACH.

We began the day fighting with midges as we dismantled our tents, throwing them into either car while stuffing our face with whatever food was readily available. Jim, Dean, Karl and Wren were ferried to Contin in the cars with John, Dave and Lyndsey. We didn't have the room for Laura.

To be fair, this was really the only time that midges had been bad (we expected worse crossing the Highlands), so we just tried moving quicker than they did. It didn't help much that both Dean and Karl were wearing a kilt.

Nicholas had driven back to join us and picked up Laura who was still at the train station car park. Jim and Dean, riding in John's car, were hoping to add some extra miles and wanted to start the journey a little further up the A835 by Rogie Falls. Dave was unwilling to change his planned start location, due to how busy and dangerous the road was for walkers during rush hour. So Dean and Jim reluctantly settled for Contin, annoying John with the indecision in planning.

Along the quieter A834, the walkers hiked along the

side of the road in what seemed like a very pleasant rural area. We walked along the road in pairs, while John stayed back, giving notice of our presence to other vehicles until we reached Strathpeffer.

Laura and Nicholas had driven ahead of us to the Deli In The Square in Strathpeffer for thirty minutes to work on essential social media and logistics. There they met Tor Justad who waxed lyrical about community and building a boat, and agreed with Laura that it was an analogy for building Scotland's civic society upwards from the grass roots. Being Scandinavian, he was amazed that Scotland hadn't already done this because Scotland has a worldwide reputation for boat building. He, and many other customers in the cafe (plus the owner), proudly took photographs with Laura wearing her 500 mile walker vest and her shield.

All the walkers noticed that Strathpeffer was a wealthy community and most likely were No voters during the 2014 referendum. Laura's interaction with the people in the deli was productive, after many showed interest in the cause and accepted leaflets promoting All Under One Banner's march in Edinburgh.

From here the walkers hiked on the footpaths which continued into Dingwall, while John in his car kept out of everyone's way. Laura and Nicholas had driven to Dingwall separately to park Nick's car and pick up coffee at Caffe Savini where organisers of Yes Ross & Sutherland met them and handed them a bundle of Yes promotion literature that they had produced.

The Yes community in Dingwall had planned a little event for our expected arrival, which was to begin at noon with a local young piper Daniel, his sister Pixie as drummer, and their mum Julie Murray, that was to lead us into Dingwall.

Nicholas and Laura rejoined us here before walking towards the town centre. Laura had walked up with the Yes Ross & Sutherland members, who were exchanging Yes badges.

The pipe band lead us past the police station, through the traffic lights into the main shopping street in town where we stopped outside the Dingwall Museum. Here we were greeted with Yes supporters who had surprised us with cupcakes. These were designed with a blue Yes logo against a white icing sugar background.

Nicholas and a local journalist interviewed Mandy Baird and Laura - both had gone to the same school and they hadn't seen each other for over 30 years. Mandy remembered Laura's class group's history of talking politics, saying "we used to have political debates on the Tomintoul school bus".

Shortly after we arrived outside the Dingwall museum, an elderly gentleman walked into the museum's side shop and photocopied a piece of unionist propaganda to hand to the local Yes group member in a silent protest before smugly slinking away. It was really a childish show of spite to watch. But it was obvious that this old gentleman was aware that we were due to arrive and that our presence was not going to go unnoticed by the unconvinced. We spent the next twenty minutes chatting with other more welcoming locals and explained why we were there.

Dingwall obviously hadn't seen much activism from the Yes movement until that day and some of the locals were visibly ecstatic that we had showed up. We didn't expect a large turnout on a Monday lunch time, but what we did see was wonderful. There were a number of people whose faces looked like we'd burned their house down, but we waved, smiled and kept on going.

Just as we were about to leave Dingwall's town centre, two young men walking with us, Darren Kenards and Patrick Robinson, indicated to Laura about the Royal Bank of Scotland, which was scheduled to be closed. They stopped for a photo with Laura and her shield with the ill-fated bank in the background.

We had all noticed one of the bank employees through an upstairs window, ecstatic at seeing us. It's sad to say that we've all been affected by bank closures in recent times, but for the smaller towns and villages across Scotland, this comes as a huge blow. It really does make you wonder why Westminster bailed out the banks, who then bailed on us when we needed them.

The walkers proceeded out of the town centre and onto Station Road heading south. We had plans to meet up with a Yes group in Beauly, so we headed that way, walking through Maryburgh, Conon Bridge and towards Muir of Ord. We took a well deserved rest when we reached the bus stops by a cross roads near The Dower House.

While taking a break, Dave received a phone call that forced him to change our plans for the day. The local MP we were expecting to meet in Inverness had a pressing time commitment. Instead of walking to Beauly, we were to be transported to Chachnaharry on the edge of Inverness, to continue walking into Inverness and meet the Yes group there.

Unfortunately the drivers of the two cars didn't communicate exactly where in Inverness we were to go and so John - after listening to Dean and Jim suggesting the easier road in to Inverness on the A9 over the Beauly Firth - got frustrated for heading the wrong way. Heated discussions ensued until we met at the edge of Inverness and got dropped off.

We continued walking along the footpaths into town where we met up with some of the local Yessers from Yes Inverness at the Telford Roundabout. From here they lead us into town and to their Yes hub in Nessie's Place on Huntly Street, overlooking the River Ness.

The Yes Inverness group had put on hot soup, rolls and cake. The local SNP MP, Drew Hendry, had cancelled his plans so he could meet and talk amongst us. Laura had been the convener of the Grantown-on-Spey branch of the SNP and had campaigned for Drew. Drew said to Laura that "You had walked non-stop 24/7 for eight months for me, so I will always walk for you". Nicholas asked for an introduction with Drew Hendry who offered 5 minutes of his time, resulting in a discussion with him about Blockchain Democracy.

The hub was full of people, many of them noticing the fatigue on our faces and that most of us had taken the brief opportunity to take our boots and shoes off for a brief respite. Just up the street, the Aye-2-Haggis catering van (the very same one we had hoped to see earlier on Skye) had setup for PR photographs with Drew. Shortly afterwards, we all gathered for photographs on the nearest pedestrian bridge over the River Ness.

We must have been in the hub for an hour or so, but we'd all lost track of time and day. Walking for so many miles, we had all got into our 'zone' and this event was no different. We were wholly reliant on Dave for keeping track of the organisation.

The plan for the rest of the day was to go to Culloden at 9pm that night and we were going to be driven there. Jim and Dean were having none of it and demanded to walk instead. So at about 7pm the Jim, Dean, Karl and Wren proceeded to walk to Culloden joined by Des Scholes, a local Yes supporter who offered to walk with us, wearing his coat blazoned with a Yes Forres logo.

We walked east through Inverness past the Raigmore Hospital and Tesco, to Culloden Road and up the hill. It had started raining and the daylight was fading, but we were as determined as we would ever be. By the time we reached the edge of the housing estates, it was pitch black and now the rain was pouring it down. We trudged on, not an umbrella between us, while John drove behind us illuminating the road and Dean using his flashing head torch for any traffic in front to see us.

We reached the locked gates of Culloden Battlefield at just after 9pm. The local supporters from Yes Inverness, Dingwall and Nairn had just ignited their torches/candles and were about to walk along the path to the battlefield with the team of walkers.

Through the pouring rain, Daniel and Pixie piped and drummed to the memorial cairn. It was starting to get quite moving and surreal; the atmosphere felt like we all had a purpose for being there. We all walked as part of a solemn procession, past the grave markers to the memorial cairn monument at the centre of the battlefield. It was here that our ceremony took place through the wind and gusts of driving rain.

Karl, an actor by trade, offered to read out a piece specially written for the event by the IndyPoet, Paul Colvin. At 9pm, in the driving rain, this is what was read:

## A Vigil Sky

*I have followed this bloodstained path you took,*
*o'er hills that you once trod*
*And I now stand in humble homage above your*
*graven sod,*
*Hear the piper in one last sweet lament, play his*
*forbidden air*
*And let the sadness fall from every note that only*
*hope can bear*

*There is no love, only death lives here, all is cold*
*and grey*
*And the mist that hides two thousand graves is*
*here again this day,*
*Its eerie silence haunts me yet I stand tall with*
*Scottish pride*
*And the tears I feel, roll down my face, are for*
*those who freely died.*

*September's vigil sky is still, and in silence, it looks*
*down,*
*Down on the dead who fell that day upon this hal-*
*lowed ground*
*And our torches tarred with blackened pitch is the*
*light they cannot see*
*For here they lie, below our feet, still hoping to be*
*free.*

*The cairns carry solemn plaques for those who*
*gave their lives*
*And though Jacobites were crushed that day, their*
*spirit still survives,*

*I stand, salute and pray for you upon this field of
death
For Jacobites you always were unto your dying
breath,*

*Lift this curse that bears them down and sweeps
Culloden Moor
And let the ghosts that cannot leave be free for
evermore.
I invoke the ancient spirits, rise, of all Culloden's
slain,
Lift this spell they've borne so long and let no guilt
there remain*

*But do not wrestle with your heart as you linger in
your grave,
Rise and lead me in my quest and show me, what
is, brave!
The pipes will guide and feed your soul and I ask
that you take part
With me upon my journey and let your heart be my
heart*

*There is so much hope, eternal, that flows through
this morbid field,
I beseech you join with me and I promise you no
yield
For I offer all I have to give if you will only walk with
me
And share in all our glory when we set our nation
free.*

*© Paul Colvin.*

It was a perfect piece for the event and was followed by a minute's silence before Daniel the piper and Pixie the drummer started up again. We were all emotional at the depth of the speech, the place, the company of like minded spirits. The challenging weather wouldn't have kept any one of us from being here.

Our driver John had become over-excited after meeting a long lost friend who was a member of Yes Inverness. As a result, he annoyed many in the gathering by talking through some of the speeches.

Afterwards we all returned to waiting vehicles, and we split up into three different teams. The local Yes Inverness family had made arrangements for places for all of us to stay for the night. This couldn't have come at a better time, since we were all soaked to the skin and many of us were given the pleasure of drying out in-front of an open fire.

Nicholas stayed with John Mellon of Yes Inverness that night. Dean, Jim, Karl, Wren and Laura stayed at Stuart MacDonald's house, who lived just down the road from Culloden. Laura had visited Stuart's house earlier to help light the fires to heat the house. Judith Reid of Yes Inverness took Dave and Lyndsey to her house.

John our driver took a wrong turn trying to find Stuart's house (where he was expected to stay) and ended up driving to and staying at Judith's house instead. Unfortunately John also had all the walkers gear, so Stuart MacDonald had to contact Judith and make arrangements to repatriate our gear. Jim offered to go with Stuart in his car to retrieve our belongings.

At this point, there had been no noticeable changes to the landscape at Culloden for the forthcoming housing development, but Jim, Laura, Wren and Karl (plus Lorna who would later be one of our drivers, Pedro Mendez and Aiden Luan a Yes Biker from Nairn that we met up with later in the walk) did return to join the protest during 13th October 2018.

# TO FORRES
## TUESDAY SEPTEMBER 18TH

None of us had any clue what day it was anymore. We just knew that we had to meet up at the Yes hub at 10am that morning so that we could walk to Forres. At Stuart MacDonald's house, Jim offered to make a full breakfast and we were much relieved that Jim was awake enough to do such a great job - the rest of us were half asleep and might have burned the house down otherwise.

We quickly discovered that John Robertson had pulled out, so we didn't have a driver that day and would have nobody to cover him for a few more. Dave hadn't planned on this and had other things that needed to be done. Nicholas wasn't made aware of the walking plan and rejoined the walkers after they had left Inverness. So we were two cars down with no lead car - the walkers would be largely on our own for a while.

John had a legitimate excuse - the disorganisation and his health issues meant he couldn't sleep. His incident at Culloden just made things really awkward. It just came at the worst possible time. It didn't help that he'd essentially let the team down - against his deepest intentions to stick together. While he knew we were all mad at him, Dean asked if "we'll see you in Edinburgh?"

Those of us who had spent the night at Stuart's house would like to thank him for his incredible hospitality and enthusiastic conversations. All our gear was dry and usable again. The Yes sign in his garden offered a great backdrop for a shield photo.

Des Scholes from Yes Nairn, who we'd met yesterday, had offered to walk with us that day, as he had walked the route before (albeit not recently). He neglected to say what the conditions were like, which was just as well as we didn't have much of a choice in the matter. But if we had, we would probably have taken alternative back roads instead - if only someone had recced the route beforehand.

Once again the weather was damp with occasional rain thrown in and didn't show much chance of getting any better for a while. But to be honest, at some point you give up caring about the weather, realising there is nothing you can do about it. We walked through damp shopping streets in Inverness, while Dean popped into Boots to stock up with more Ibuprofen and a bottle of water that he'd forgotten to bring along (distributing 500 miles badges for the cashiers). We walked to the edge of town, alongside the wall of the train lines towards the A9 intersection with the A96. There were a few waves and cheers as we walked past some local builders. Obviously word of our endeavour was getting out.

When we made it to the A96, we were surprised to discover there was a very well used footpath, beside this extremely busy road. Two miles in however, the sign for *Milton of Culloden* marked where pedestrians were no longer invited or even tolerated. This was already looking like it would be a long day ahead.

We would soon discover that we would have had to endure another ten miles walking alongside this busy single-carriageway road until the next footpath was to welcome our feet. We walked on the road whenever we could, reverting to the grass verge whenever a bus, lorry or emergency vehicle was approaching. Dean wore a flashing lamp on his head to try to warn passing traffic, but that didn't prevent some motorists almost running us off the road. Our problem was that the side of the road was completely uneven, and we knew that walking on it both slowed us down and made our feet more prone to blisters. Laura ended up twisting her ankle along that stretch.

A short while later, Laura's ankle pain and the lack of a driver on this stretch meant she couldn't keep up the pace the rest of us were walking. She really needed a break and some assistance. We all needed to get off this road as quickly as possible as it was obviously a dangerous route to walk. Since we had no backup car, the only option was to catch the bus from Inverness. Des said there would be a bus shortly that would take Laura directly to the bus station in Nairn. Laura crossed the road to wait for the bus while the rest of us continued on.

Shortly afterwards, the bus to Nairn arrived and the driver instantly recognised that Laura was a 500 mile walker, noticing her difficulty walking and offering her free passage to Nairn.

The rest of the walkers trudged along the side of the road. At one point, we came across a recent crash scene with police tape surrounding the two separate cars. The first was overturned in a ditch and the other was 200 yards further down the highway, with both doors smashed in on one side. Quite a sobering sight to see when you are a pedestrian. We plodded on.

We soon heard aircraft overhead, which meant we were getting close to Inverness Airport. At Tornagrain near the Petty Church we spotted an entrance to a tree farm, with trees stacked in a way that would make a good secluded spot to eat our sandwiches. We stopped briefly, enjoying the smell of fresh cut wet pine. It was a pleasant break from the relentless traffic.

We continued on along the 10 miles of path-less road, but noticed that the churned up mud on the side of the road had receded. Des mentioned that was due to the fact that we'd passed Norbord - the wood processing plant where all the timber lorries were going.

Surprisingly we now had a clear view of the edge of the road and there were now places for the rainwater to go. We somehow had at least an extra foot of roadside to use, and at some points there was a visible white stripe with space on the outside for us to walk on! How strange that this was quickly considered a blessing. It made us wonder, how much mud had all these timber lorries left beside the road to build up?

At some point along this section, Lyndsey was dropped off by Nicholas while he continued to drive into Nairn. We got back into the zone and plodded on a mostly straight stretch. In the distance was an uplifting sight - a couple of supporters with Yes Saltires, Alison and John Nicol, were waiting for us at Carnach House. For a few miles, we walked at a much more leisurely pace as we approached Nairn, only to see the blue sky appear, joined by blinding sun. This was the half way point for the day, yet we were already exhausted.

Nairn has a little art/garden installation alongside the road, which was perfect for a spot for us to sit and have lunch. Des had provided us with sandwiches and brought bottled water and chocolate biscuits! He offered to take Wren to his house nearby to freshen up. The rest of us just spent the time enjoying the unexpected break.

Laura, who had taken the bus to Nairn earlier had stopped in the Co-op opposite the bus station while waiting for Nicholas to arrive. There she met James Jack and Stuart MacPhee who were raising money for Hospice Nairn. They recognised Laura's 500miles vest, wanting a photograph with her and offered to publish information about us, to their local Facebook friends. Laura took notes of people she met while waiting for the other walkers: Shaun Wemyss in Trespass, Wendy Burnett, Iain Bruce, Alison & John Nicol (and their dog Rex), Sean, Margaret, Ann and Emma.

Nicholas had driven to Nairn, taking the opportunity to meet up with Laura and grab a cup of coffee while waiting for the remaining walkers to arrive.

The remaining walkers continued hiking into Nairn town centre where they met up with Dave. Dave had parked in a car park opposite the Co-op waiting for us. Here, Nicholas and Laura then rejoined the walkers, hiking down Leopold Street onto High Street, where everyone stopped for a break outside the town hall.

Aidan McCormack, one of the Yes Bikers and activist with Yes Nairn, had stopped by to meet us and give us a donation. Laura had a photograph taken with him holding her shield while sitting on the back of his parked bike. Aiden was a huge activist, passionate for the underdog and a musician, well known in Highlands.

Sadly Aidan passed away suddenly on the following Boxing day. We all send our condolences to his wife Luan and children.

We continued on, stopping briefly at the studio of Marc Marnie - the pleasantly eccentric local photographer. Inside his shop, on the wall above the front window is a big old fashioned golden "Yes" sign. We said our hellos, while Nicholas got a photo with Marc, and we were all wished the best of luck.

Nicholas asked if anyone could drive his car to Forres so he could walk with the team for a while. Laura with her ankle pain was happy to oblige, driving Nicholas' car to the Tesco car park at Forres to meet up with us later. In Forres, Laura met with Aoibhinn Doran, one of the managers at Tesco, about the walk and took a photograph with Aoibhinn, holding the shield.

The walkers continued out of Nairn to our final destination for the day. Des fortunately knew a much quieter road to get to Forres, which stuck to the general direction we wanted to go. After crossing the River Nairn we took Lochloy Road and headed through Kingsteps.

The difference in the walking route was night-and-day, compared with the first half of the day. No longer struggling alongside a busy road, this was pleasantly refreshing. A jogger passed us along the way, only to re-appear jogging in the same direction a few miles later. We were bewildered as to how. We hiked along the back roads and onto country paths, past farms and back on country roads via the Broom of Moy. It was here where a footbridge crossed the River Findhorn which bewilderingly lead into an industrial estate and onwards directly into Forres itself.

Since there was no car following us today, Dave was using the GPS locations shared from Dean's mobile phone. Dave used it to meet up with the walkers on a couple of occasions when hiking along the country roads. In between visits, Dave and Lyndsey had taken the opportunity to pick up supplies from nearby shops.

Knowing where the walkers were headed, he also coordinated with the group of Yes supporters from Forres. They would meet the walkers at the edge of the park, on the footpath that lead to the Lidl store in Forres. It was extremely rewarding for the walkers to meet the group after such a long day. The sunlight was quickly fading and we were happy to make it to our destination town before the sky was completely dark.

In Forres, the group meandered and split up but headed for High Street where everyone stopped for an impromptu photo-shoot outside the office of Douglas Ross MP. There we took a photograph with four "Yes" Saltire flags in full view. It seemed oddly out of character that the Scottish Conservative & Unionist MP would be based here in Forres.

We then discovered that nobody had made any plans for where the walkers were to eat or sleep for the night. Officially we'd walked more than a marathon that day - a total of 27.5 miles. The walkers were feeling far too exhausted to do anything more. The local Yes group hadn't been consulted about accommodation, so they had no idea what we would require.

Jim and Dean left the discussion after spotting that the local chip shop was still open at 9pm. They were not going to wait and pass up the opportunity. Some of the others did the same since the choices nearby were dwindling by the minute. We were thankful that the chip shop had an area to sit down and a toilet.

Dave suggested we camp out in the local park as the weather was about to turn, so Jim and Dean setup camp while Dave and Lyndsey planned on sleeping in the car on the street nearby.

Prior to this trip, none us would have chosen to camp out like this, and we honestly wouldn't have done it given an opportunity to do otherwise. But based on the time frame and the fact that we were mentally and physically exhausted, Jim and Dean didn't even question the idea, and simply setup their tents.

Laura, Karl and Wren were not comfortable with the sleeping arrangements, understandably expecting there to be something better planned. Laura knew this area well and knew of a nearby camp site. She had Dave retrieve gear from his car for herself, Wren and Karl, transferring it into Nicholas' car. Unfortunately, due to the chaotic change of moving everything from John's car into Dave's car and then into Nicholas' car, it meant they would all discover some part of their gear was missing in the disarray.

Jim, in tired confusion, took over a half hour to setup his tent in Grant Park, grateful that Dean had brought a bright lamp to assist in the process. Both Jim's and Dean's tents were setup before the weather front hit with a large blast of wind and rain. They were both pitched under a row of large old trees that still had their leaves, so they were both protected from the worst of the weather. Unfortunately the only public toilet nearby appeared to be located in the community centre, and that didn't open until 8am the following day.

The walkers at the camp-site were not so lucky with the weather, setting up camp in the middle of the rain storm. There was an air of frustrated tension at the Forres Camp site, alleviated somewhat with a couple of nips of whisky. An exhausted Karl J Claridge was in hysterical laughter after Nicholas crept up outside his tent, and started playing the Benny Hill theme tune music on his portable speaker!

Frustration with lack of planning was starting to take it's toll. The hike wasn't necessarily the hardest part for the walkers. The fact that we'd been repeatedly left to our own devices did not bode well. We had hoped something was going to change, and soon. Still we wondered - where were we sleeping tomorrow and what would we eat?

# ELGIN THEN FOCHABERS
## WEDNESDAY SEPTEMBER 19TH

The day started with the party split in two. Jim was up at the crack of dawn as if he'd just finished army basic training - no small feat considering he'd just recently retired. Dean wasn't far behind, and at this point he and Jim had really become good friends. Both tents were packed and stowed in Dave's car before 8am when they both proceeded to visit the Forres Community Centre and freshen up.

They picked up some energy-rich snack food from Dave's car, topped up water bottles and headed off for Elgin. With the exception of the road out of Forres, the rest of the trip into Elgin would be along the A96. Fortunately this morning's traffic wasn't nearly as bad as the previous section. The dry spell of weather seemed to be holding on by a thread. There were large sections where the side of the road was reasonably walk-able without resorting to hiking on the uneven grass. Compared to yesterday morning, it hardly looked like we were walking on a stretch of the same road.

Jim and Dean hiked for nearly five miles before being joined by Wren, Karl and Laura who had been given a lift to that point to catch up. At this point, with all the disruption, we had to look at this as a team effort, making sure that most of us would cover the distance.

The road here was still very accommodating to walkers, and we were happy to see a stretch of footpath to use when we reached Alves. Unfortunately it was short-lived. The other side of town had about a foot and a half of tarmac and gravel for us to use.

Before reaching Elgin, we came across a wooded area and he verge of the road had got thinner again. We had lost the option to do anything but walk on the side of the road itself. We kept on walking in single file until we reached a few old-fashioned buildings alongside the road. Here one of the Yes supporters from Elgin had driven ahead on his covered bike. He was flying the Saltire for our arrival. It seems such a little thing, but at that point it was a wonderful sight to see, having walked miles and seen little of any significance until then. We stopped for a brief chat, but were told there was a party of people waiting for us in Elgin, so we continued on.

On the approach into Elgin, the stands of trees fall away and we could see a dozen or so people proudly flying flags in the distance alongside the Elgin town sign. Passing cars were also honking at us as we hiked towards town. It was oddly electric and given the lack of planning to date, it was quite unexpected.

After a quick meet and greet, we were told we needed to keep walking, following the group into the town centre. We crossed the roundabout, happily leaving the A96 onto South Street, walking to Thunderton Place and around the corner to a restaurant called "Scribbles".

The local SNP group had put on a lunch for us here,

so we graciously accepted and had an hour's break. Scribbles is a very pleasant Italian restaurant, and we were joined by a number of councillors including the local SNP councillor Paula Coy and Buckie branch SNP member Graeme Goodall, both offering donations to help towards the walkers expenses.

Paula Coy late Tweeted: "So great to meet all the people doing the #500MilesWalk today! Their passion is an inspiration!"

There we met Tarya, a young lady who wanted to join us for the next section of the walk and was happy to be our local expert for the rest of the day. We really had no idea just how important her role would become.

Laura and Nicholas left in the car with lots of gear. Nicholas had an appointment with a deadline in Fife, so his time was short, joking that Laura had ten minutes to get our accommodation sorted.

With the use of social media, Laura made arrangements and almost immediately received a response from Barry and Bernadette. They had recently lost a family member who was an avid Indy supporter and offered the walkers the use of their camp-site. That day was also the anniversary of the 2014 Scottish independence referendum. Barry and Bernadette found solace from their grief by helping the walkers, seeing them as an inspiration.

Once the gear was dropped off and Nicholas had left to return to Fife, Laura wanted to walk out to meet the walkers. Unfortunately Dave hadn't had the chance to share the walkers location with her. So Laura patiently waited at the camp-site in Fochabers.

The walkers continued down Elgin's High Street and rejoined the footpath of the A96 to the edge of town.

Before exiting the town limits, the walkers took a left turn at the roundabout by KFC and the dead-end road turned into a gorgeous walking/cycling path that headed the same direction as the A96 but much more scenic.

We walked into Lhanbryde, and tried to find a toilet to use. The local Spar supermarket was the only option as the community toilets appear to have been permanently shuttered. It was disheartening to see the village main street look so bleak. Was this all due to the toll from years of austerity?

As we were leaving Lhanbryde, we were presented with a wonderful full arched rainbow in the distance. This remained as we rejoined a path along the A96. The path quite simply stopped in the middle of nowhere - as they strangely tend to do - only to restart again almost two miles later - seemingly in the middle of nowhere. Since we were walking on the opposite side of the road to the path, we didn't even notice it re-starting until a lorry honked at us. The sporadic path game was now starting to become a running joke. You do wonder, who makes plans for building a footpath along a major highway that runs along only 90% of the route? Why do they bother to start, if they ultimately go nowhere?

The Mosstodloch turn off from the A96 couldn't have come soon enough. We were able to walk through Mosstodloch, past the Baxters plant and on a footpath and subway under the A96. There we crossed a bridge that ran alongside the A96. Presumably this was how staff from Fochabers could walk to work at the Baxters plant - how civilised!

When we got to the other side of the bridge, we couldn't see around the corner for the trees. You can imagine our surprise to be greeted by Tarya's parents who happened to be the same couple who had offered us lodging for the night. Laura, Dave and Lyndsey and other family members were also there to greet us as we walked into Fochabers. Barry and Bernie had driven over with their grandchildren. They were so happy to have photographs taken while we shared our hi-visibility vests for the kids to wear while flying a saltire for a little while.

Here we walked all the way along High Street in Fochabers, until eventually reaching the Burnside Caravan Site. Barry and Bernie managed the camp site and offered the use of their community room to use as one big 'bedroom'.

There was an offer for us to use their swimming pool which had already been closed for the season. We declined their generous offer, as what we really needed was dinner and a good night's sleep. Fish 'n Chips were ordered, and Jim offered to help our hosts pickup the orders. The rest of us tried to reunite our individual gear so we would have some kind of order. This was also a perfect opportunity to patch up our ailing feet and use the free Wi-Fi to get our updates with the outside world.

Mary Jenkins had also told local Yes supporters about our plans to stop the night at the camp ground. Nicholas had also tweeted the same information earlier. Thanks to this, a number of local supporters came to visit us and offered donations of first aid supplies, food and drinks for our onward travels. We'd like to thank Jane Loveland, Indy Bikers David and Viki, Vicky Stewart, Mary and Graham Jenkins, Mary Jenkins, Julie Harris, Barbera and Douglas and Ed for all their generosity.

Robert and Liz Knight from Port Gordon of the Elgin AGM group also stopped to see us in Fochabers, bringing us a bag of food and whisky and took time to speak with Laura. Robert offered to move all our gear to the next day's endpoint, which was a huge boon as we'd been reduced to one car for transporting gear. Laura arranged the logistics with them, without actually knowing where that location would be! Robert also generously offered to move our gear for another jump the following day.

Although some of us were up until midnight, we've no idea where our time went. But we were warm, dry, fed and physically recharged for more. We had use of the nicest toilets and showers since the start, and our hosts were absolutely wonderful. Thank you so much!

# THE LONG WAY TO BANFF
## THURSDAY SEPTEMBER 20TH

We had packed up our belongings and for most of us it was the first time since leaving Skye that we had found the opportunity to consolidate everything that each of us had brought. Wren still couldn't find her bank card, and reported it lost.

We took group photographs with our hosts and packed some of our gear into Dave's car. The lack of choices with transportation was beginning to wear thin and Dave wanted to walk again. His feet had finally recovered from the swelling and blisters from the first day on Skye. Lyndsay had helped him pick better footwear and socks to get Dave ready to go.

Laura stopped behind to sort out the remainder of our gear, arranging accommodation for the coming night and chose to do the same for the next stage.

The rest of us left the camp site, and turned right at the roundabout up to another roundabout. Here we didn't continue on the A96, but instead took the A98 (coast road) which immediately led us into a wooded area. The traffic levels were not particularly pleasant to walk alongside, so at the first opportunity we quickly decided to take the smaller back roads instead.

This route offered relief but came with the caveat that the roads were full of bends and steep hills which would delay us getting to our destination. We were surprised to meet up again with Julie Harris (who had visited us at the camp-site the previous night) when we reached Clochan. We presumed that Dave must have told her our whereabouts, based on tracking Dean's location. She and her two dogs walked with us, up to the Women's Land Army Memorial (which recognises the women drafted to work the fields, while the men were off to war during the First and Second World Wars).

We stopped to take some photographs before we continued on towards the historical site of St. Gregory's Church. Shortly afterwards Julie bid us farewell as she walked her dogs towards their home while we continued along the road that descended into and up the other side of the glen.

This was beautiful countryside and full of character. But by the time we approached Drybridge, we knew we were losing valuable time due to the winding hilly roads.

Dave and Lyndsey later drove by the walkers to give updates. We already knew we couldn't hack any more of the back roads and headed back onto towards the A98 near Buckie.

Once back on the main road, we headed north easterly, towards Cullen. Earlier, Dave forewarned us of two things. Cullen is a fishing town where we would need to descend down to sea level before returning back up the hill. Cullen is obviously famous as the home of Cullen Skink (which you can occasionally smell in the air as you approach town), but also famous for their local ice cream shop.

To be honest, the walkers were hoping that Dave, Lyndsey and Laura would be meeting us in town, ready for a bite of lunch and ice cream, but that wasn't to be.

Laura, Robert and Liz had driven ahead and tried to get a quote for the team at the Banff Links Caravan Park, temporarily getting a key from the manager, Georgina, to store the luggage in their laundry room. They then drove on the Spotty Bag Shop to meet up with Dave and Lyndsey.

At the Spotty Bag Shop, the shop staff were surprised and excited to see Laura, wearing a 500 mile walker vest entering their shop. They all wanted photographs with her vest and shield. Laura met and talked with Donald Thain, the manager. They discussed the ancient Thain clan, being extremely proud of their Scottish heritage and their appreciation of the Yes movement. He urgently wanted Scottish independence most for his wife, due to her ailing health.

Dave and Lyndsey arrived at the Spotty Bag Shop a hour after Laura, telling her that they had booked a place at the more sheltered Myrus Holiday Park in Macduff.

The unannounced change in plans, had become a last straw for Laura. She never expected to take on the organisation for accommodation and donations, and demanded some clarity and peace. There at the restaurant table, they made up their differences, hugged and worked out plans as a team.

The walkers, back in Cullen reached the famous Ice Cream shop, but some walkers needed to take a loo break. Since it was no longer summer tourist season, the public toilets were locked. It just happened that the owner of The Ice Cream Shop was walking towards the walkers and offered them the key. Afterwards we all headed to The Ice Cream Shop and indulged in their ice cream, a cup of fresh coffee and bought some of their old fashioned sweets. The owner, a lady from Liverpool, was no fan of independence, but was friendly and had no problem refilling our water bottles and hearing about our endeavour.

The ice cream made us hungry, and we quickly discovered that Cullen is a bit of a sleepy town on Thursdays. It was fortunate that the newsagents had a couple packs of sandwiches remaining to sell. We reached the top of the glen out of Cullen where we found a stone wall of perfect height to have a "quick" rest. We must have sat there for half a hour before continuing, after waiting for the energy from eating all the food to finally kick in.

This was where we began to take note of the fact that in addition to being deficient in footpaths, Scotland also has barely any benches to sit on. There is a bench or two in Cullen where people catch the bus. But there's few located where you'd like to actually sit and look at the gorgeous view across the countryside.

For now, we were grateful to see a footpath out of Cullen. Strangely the footpath started to veer off the A96 onto what must have been the old road before it was diverted onto a easier route. In the middle of this off-shoot path was a car park. There we met a man who must have been in contact with Dave, as he knew we were passing through and wished us well on our trek.

Following the old footpath lead us into a wood and a dead end. We headed back towards the main road by walking through a gate to get back to the A96. Shortly as we crossed into Aberdeenshire, the footpath disintegrated. We all wondered aloud - how could Aberdeenshire (home to the oil businesses) not afford to continue a footpath on their second busiest road? Harrumph.

It wasn't long before we got back into the zone, walking in single file along the side of the busy road, yielding to large vehicles as we had done earlier. The traffic seemed to quieten down as we passed Glenglassaugh Distillery and all thought wonderful thoughts about taking a 'brief' detour. But in pure determination to get to Banff today, we kept going.

Jim was hoping on taking a quick rest for a few minutes at the bus shelter which had a bench, but neither Wren nor Karl could hear Jim or Dean call to stop. Karl had walked ahead of Wren on his own and Dean ran ahead to ask him to stop for a break and advise him that walking ahead alone wasn't particularly safe. Karl had an outburst of anger over something and Dean didn't understand why. Karl and Wren had become inseparable friends, but something had upset him. Wren urged Dean to leave Karl alone. Confused, Dean left them both and walked back to take a five minutes break in the bus shelter with Jim.

Wren and Karl made up their differences and slowed down, while Jim and Dean soon caught up and gave them a little distance to stay in front. For a short while it felt awkward, but we had a job to do and plodded on.

Just before we got to Portsoy, we came across a lay-by where two unfamiliar cars seemed to be waiting for us. A woman with a camera and an oddly large lens got out the first car we passed and we assume she had simply used it to take pictures of us along the road.

The younger woman from the second car seemed

pleased to see us and asked where Dave was.

We all thought her question seemed oddly presented, as not exactly friendly. Nevertheless we took her photograph and Wren offered her the opportunity to ring the freedom bell - which she did. Whether these women were friend or foe, we were not there to argue nor ask for money. We parted after saying goodbye, but continued to feel that something was very odd about the encounter.

Long after the walk was completed we discovered that the second woman was indeed no friend to our cause. In fact, she is quite an outspoken unionist on social media. How ironic that she had rung our freedom bell!

An image on a YouTube profile perfectly matched the woman we met. We noticed it in a post that denied controversial behaviour of flag-waving unionists at a pro-independence event the following year. It seems quite likely now, that these two women from Aberdeenshire used the camera to spy on us for a good portion of our 500 miles walk and used it to report our location.

The landscape in these parts seemed to be noticeably more affluent, no doubt thanks to the oil fortunes across Aberdeenshire. But what was evident was how many people noticed us. As we got closer to Banff, the number of people who were visibly offended by our presence increased dramatically. Obviously the local unionists had been tipped off. Now more than ever we could have done with a support driver. Dean sent a text message to Dave that something had changed.

For safety sake, the team stayed together for the rest of the route. Oddly we'd seen a sign that said "Banff - 5 miles". We were somewhat upbeat about nearing the end before coming across yet another sign that said "Banff - 5 miles"! We must have already walked a mile or so before that second sign! This was becoming the longest five miles ever.

The walkers took a break at the turn off for Aberchirder / Turriff and sat alongside the bus stop. We were physically knackered. Some of us laid down in the grass for five minutes to recover. We theoretically had just under five miles left that day. If it had started raining, I suspect we'd still be at that bus stop.

Dave was waiting for us in the lay-by by the northern entrance into Banff - our 25.5mile mark. He'd been watching the social media channels and thought, for our own safety, that we shouldn't try walking through Banff - especially with our vests advertising who we were.

Our odd encounter at the lay-by earlier must have made it to social media, and made us appear much too vulnerable for our own good. He'd realised from the negative reactions from passing traffic, that we were really going to need much more protection if we were to make it through Aberdeenshire without an incident. Dave had called in the help from some of his friendly Yes Biker friends who offered to join us as soon as they could.

We walked all the way to the Banff road sign and Dean took more photographs of the gorgeous setting sun behind us, showing the windmills to the west. We all jumped into Dave's car parked in the lay-by, to be driven into town. The car was mostly empty as he'd unloaded it at the camp site nearby, so we'd all fit in. Before driving to our base camp, we were taken to a local fast food shop in Banff where Dave ordered whatever dinner each of us wanted from the menu.

After waiting for our food to be cooked, we headed back to the camp-site, where we were staying for the night. It was dark when we got to the Myrus Holiday Park in Macduff. The owners had let us use their out-buildings for the night. We had heat and light, but no electricity. Fortunately Dean had brought a huge battery backup/charger he uses for mobile photography lighting, that had already helped along the way for keeping our mobile phones alive.

From the dry warmth of the laundry room, we had our first conference call with Pilar Fernandez of Rosalía TV, in Galicia. We were all in the room when the first two walkers, Wren Chapman and Jim Stewart were interviewed for Pilar's show (available at pilaraymara. com - September 21st 2018 in the "Arquive").

We charged up whatever we could with the battery charger before going to bed. It finally ran out of juice while Laura was doing work on her laptop. Most of us camped out in our tents again that night. Dave and Lyndsey slept in the car while Laura slept in the warm and dry laundry room (trying not to move, as that would trigger the motion sensor lights to switch on!).

It rained again. So much for "red sky at night". The tent dwellers didn't take long to fall asleep, the light drizzle helping to drown out any noise. Even in what felt a little like enemy territory, we still felt calm and safe.

Whilst we had been walking, we were completely unaware that MSP Jenny Gilruth had lodged a motion in the Scottish Parliament (Motion S5M-14041), which commends the 500 miles walkers and their promotion of electoral reform through Blockchain technology.

**Motion S5M-14041: Jenny Gilruth, Mid Fife and Glenrothes, Scottish National Party, Date Lodged: 20/09/2018**

**Nicholas Russell's 500-mile Walk**

That the Parliament commends the efforts of Nicholas Russell, the owner of the Balbirnie House Hotel in Markinch, and five other volunteers, for preparing to embark on a 500-mile walk, beginning at Portree and ending in Edinburgh, in a bid to bring attention to electoral reform; understands that the volunteers hope that the introduction of blockchain technology will provide a basis for wider voter participation in Scotland and could prove crucial in any future votes on issues such as Brexit and a second independence referendum; notes that the 500-mile walk was opened by Ian Blackford MP on 15 September 2018 and is expected to end on 6 October at the Parliament, and wishes all of the volunteers the best of luck on the rest of the journey.

**Supported by:** Joan McAlpine, David Torrance, Richard Lyle, Bill Kidd, Fulton MacGregor, Mark Ruskell, Clare Adamson, Tom Arthur

# THE HELLISH ROAD TO HEAVEN
## FRIDAY SEPTEMBER 21ST

NÍ HÉ LÁ NA BÁISTÍ LÁ NA BPÁISTÍ.

Friday wasn't just another day. We awoke to a damp, driech morning. The tents were soaking wet through. Getting changed into walking gear in the heated toilet next to the laundry, Dean realized it would have made for a great room to sleep. In hindsight, starting off warm and dry would likely have helped our spirits later that morning.

The wind had picked up but the weather wasn't looking to improve anytime soon. Until now, none of the walkers had paid very much attention to the weather. It wasn't as if we could do anything about it. It was what it was, and we simply trudged through it akin to a group of soldiers. Our single goal was to get to Edinburgh. Storm Aileen on Skye was behind us. Surely nothing could beat that? We just sensed it was going to be a wet day and dressed for that scenario.

After picking up our damp camping gear, Dave drove the walkers to our starting point. We were dropped off at the intersection where the bridge to Banff ends and Macduff begins. We walked the footpath along the A98 by the seafront and on into the fishing town of Macduff.

Laura had waited behind to talk to John Ritchie,
the owner of the Myrus Holiday Park. She wanted to
discuss the local issues regarding fishing and farming
(John had wisely bought the camp site using his
investments from exiting from the fishing industry).
John was interested in Laura's views on the lack of
investment in local towns and the issues surrounding
the relationship with the rest of the UK. Laura was
happy to see someone from a heavy unionist area who
was so open to discussion. It seemed like local minds
could be changed.

Macduff seemed like a typical fishing town as the
walkers passed through it. We walked up the brae
where we soon came across Neil Cameron, a Yes
supporter that lived near Fraserburgh. He offered to be
our local expert and guide for the day and unlike the
rest of us, Neil looked like he'd paid some attention to a
weather forecasts with all his waterproofs.

Before leaving Macduff, Neil pointed out a large
Saltire that had been prominently nailed onto the
side of a house. He told us that the owner was not
a Scottish nationalist, but instead was a prominent
supporter of the union with England. At least the owner
respected that this flag represented their own country,
conscientiously choosing that over the union flag. We'd
like to think of it as a small step in the right direction.

We continued to the top of the fishing town and back
into the countryside again. As usual, the footpath ended
at an industrial estate at the edge of town. Fortunately
we didn't have far to go before our turn off onto the
B9031 towards Fraserburgh.

At this point, it had been raining and windy but then
the heavens opened. It was the kind of weather where
drivers enjoying a dry seat in a car would have had

the wipers going full speed and possibly slowing down because they don't work fast enough.

If a support vehicle had been available, many of us would have considered taking breaks. But that simple luxury wasn't there. It could not have been a mile along the coast road with the wind and driving rain, before most of us were thoroughly drenched to the skin. Our socks weren't much dryer either.

You can imagine our surprise when two local Yes supporters - Alan Gow and Peter Geddes - chose that point to begin to walk with us. They had intended walking with us for a couple of miles or so. But after less than half that, thoroughly drenched themselves, they chose to turn back to return to their car. We couldn't blame them as we would have done the same.

Dave stopped by in the dry car to offer us anything we wanted. At that point, we were beyond help. Dean dropped off his camera in the car to keep it safe until our next meeting point. This was the only time along the entire route when he didn't carry his DSLR camera. Fortunately it was rainproof and is still working like a champ.

Near St. Johns Churchyard is a relatively steep double bend that also has a dip in the middle. The rain was starting to let up at this point but the roads were soaking wet. It was here where we nearly encountered a major incident.

Based on the traffic, there must have been a classic car show somewhere nearby. Almost every car passing us heading towards Banff was at least forty years old. As one of the cars drove down the brae into the glen much too quickly, they noticed us walking uphill on the right side with our hi-vis vests and started to brake hard. Recall the noise of squealing brakes in the American cop shows in the 1970's and you get the idea. The car managed to slow down before reaching us, but it made us wonder if we would be so lucky with the next one. The squealing car must have been a green 1970s Ford Cortina or similar. The next car was at least 20 years older than that. No surprise that we were relieved to get past that curvy stretch of road without an accident. Thank heavens for hi-vis vests.

The rain finally stopped, but the gale force winds kept blowing in from the sea. Shortly afterwards the sky cleared and when we reached the entrance to Troup House School, we decided it was an opportune moment for a refuelling break. Neil had brought sandwiches, fruit and snack bars for us. We really needed the energy to keep our core warm, as the wind wasn't letting off. Luckily it was drying us out - except for our boots which for most of us were now squelchy and damp. There was nowhere to sit, so we had no choice but stand around until we were all done eating.

The next section of the walk was through some truly gorgeous scenery - wonderfully unspoiled. We walked by the Mill of Nethermill. Neil told us that it was owned by a retired couple who moved from South Carolina, USA to start a self catering business here - a truly beautiful spot to stay if you get the opportunity. Jim was excited to tell us about Pennan, the town where "Local Hero" was filmed (the location called "Ferness" in the film), which we would soon pass the side road to.

The last four miles before reaching New Aberdour were extremely hilly and full of bends. We were honestly exhausted by the time we got there. We were amazed to be received into town by two guardian angels and their four legged friends.

Jan and John Reekie lead us to their house, fed us

home-made soup, plus tea, coffee and offers of whisky. We couldn't possibly have thanked them enough after the way the day had gone so far. We finally had an opportunity to take off our boots and dry our socks and boots. We felt spoiled - it was both awesome and humbling.

Laura who was in the car with Robert and Liz Knight, had no idea where we had stopped in New Aberdour, driving back and forth along the road before stopping in Pennan for photographs with the shield at the famous phone-box from Local Hero (like Jim had wanted to do but fortunately didn't, due to the extremely steep road back to the coast road which would have been brutal). Afterwards, not knowing where to meet up with Dave or the walkers and needing to leave themselves, Robert and Liz continued driving to Fraserburgh. They dropped off Laura and the excess gear that didn't fit in Dave's car at the local Asda there.

The walkers back in New Aberdour found it sad to leave so soon, and Jan Reekie showed us their newly renovated and prized bus stop covered in wonderful Scottish symbolism. In a land where the Scottish cringe undercurrent is often present, this was a glowing sign of relief.

Neil kept the walkers going along the road towards Fraserburgh, but we took an alternate route in order to avoid any unnecessary contact with the A98. We hiked onto the B9031, then took the right turn towards Peethill - following the track road until we approached the B9031 again by the sea - just south of Sandhaven. We were surprised to be joined again by Alan, Peter and now Dave as we all proceeded to walk towards a large crowd of people at the end of the B9031 in Fraserburgh.

Before getting to the end of the road, we passed the

Asda where Laura had stopped with the second carload of gear. Laura legged it to the embankment to wave at us, speaking to Dean who was taking photographs at the back of the walking pack. We couldn't pickup Laura, as all the support vehicles had already been parked behind us.

Reaching the end of the road in Fraserburgh, it seemed like everyone was carrying a flag, sign or something to show their appreciation. Dave had made sure that Yes supporters in Fraserburgh knew when we were expected to arrive. It was here that saw our first printed #500miles sign and felt immensely proud for what we had already accomplished. The walkers didn't expect this kind of reception.

We were lead with a piper into town to stop at the local Cheers Cafe, Bar and Tavern where Angie Gibson, Morag Richie and Neil Cameron of the local Yes group had put on a buffet and bought all the 500 mile team a drink. Thank you to Dennis Forsyth, Yes supporter and owner of Cheers Bar, for hosting this gathering.

Lots of Yes cup cakes had been made for the event. We all thoroughly enjoyed our time there, and honestly we couldn't have wished for more. It was unfortunate that we were so worn out from the 23 miles hiked that day. I think we were all too shell shocked to talk much. Getting out of the zone and socialising takes time.

Pre-planning hadn't happened regarding the sleeping arrangements. Neil Cameron put us up in his house and offered us anything we needed. We don't know how we could have made it that day without him.

Laura, still at the Fraserburgh Asda, was trying to figure out how to reconnect with us. At Neil's house, Dean realised the odd disconnect with Laura and some of our gear. Neil offered to pickup Laura and bring her back to his house.

We should mention that while three of us were born in England, the others were born and raised in Scotland. Alan Gow - who we were introduced to that day as "Doric Alan", was one of the unexpected highlights of the day. Dean (Yorkshire born and raised but had also lived in the United States for decades thanks in part to lack of jobs under Margaret Thatcher) had photographed and documented numerous Scottish historical projects revolving around the Doric and Scots languages, but had never conversed with someone who actually spoke full-on Doric before. To say it came as a bit of a shock would be an understatement. Alan never tired of the questioning looks on our faces and just beamed a smile. If you're reading this Alan, *ta mucklie fer joinin us toonsers*. And to Peter Geddes, thank you for walking with us whilst helping to translate.

Thank you to everyone in Fraserburgh and New Aberdour for offering us your hearts and so much more.

This was the end of the first week. While we hadn't actually walked every mile from Skye (and realistically couldn't), we *had* walked almost the entire way from Inverness to Fraserburgh and a total of 142 miles walked so far. Some of us had to be reminded that the point was not to cover every mile of road - but primarily to engage with Yes groups, to connect them all along the way, to engage with people to show our positive message for an independent Scotland. So far, so good.

During the evening, we did what we could to recover our poor feet. Jim was somehow immune to issues with his feet. The rest of us were starting to wonder what magic he was privy to. Wren, Karl, Dean and Laura had blisters of varying degrees, and nothing was really helping. Compeed plasters are a godsend, but only when you can take the time off to stop re-creating the problem in the first place. We all quickly became experts at treating blisters, but realised what we really needed was free time to recover. We will spare everyone the gory details of our toenails.

We'd surprised ourselves getting this far and perhaps being out of touch on social media helped us along the way. We had only heard from others about the fallout on social media from our presence in some very Conservative-leaning areas.

We intentionally chose to ignore the cringe-riddled negativity and embrace positive change. We weren't willing to be beaten! And surely the worst that mother nature could dish out was behind us?

We discovered late that night that our social media presence was seen by hundreds of thousands of people already. That day it included an offer of a large donation from Julie Bond in Canada! We would have gladly accepted, but the organisers still had issues with setting up a merchant Paypal account - sadly something that would never get resolved.

Nicholas, continuing to work on his #BlockchainDemocracy project, received a call from Gordon Macintyre-Kemp, CEO of Business for Scotland, who sent 'Thoughts and best wishes with all in and around project #500miles'. He had received confirmation from a blockchain academic that funding would be made available for the Scottish Common Blockchain.

# FAMOUS IN PETERHEAD
## SATURDAY SEPTEMBER 22ND

Saturday morning seemed like it was going to be a pleasant day. We were walking to Peterhead, before heading for Ellon. We knew we had a meeting with Gillian Martin MSP along the way, but otherwise little else was planned that we were aware of.

The day started off outside Neil Cameron's house. Laura and Dave wanted to have photo's taken with his restored Clan Cameron claymore sword he was so proud of. Due to time constraints, he had to bring it with him to get images at the starting point.

Then we all left in a convoy of vehicles towards Lonmay, our starting point. From there it was a more manageable twenty-eight mile stretch to Ellon. The drop-off location was just after a split in the A90, where most of the local traffic would take the A952 instead, leaving us with much lower traffic levels and fewer irate drivers.

Today we were joined by Andrew Stewart Murray, who was happy to walk alongside us for the whole day. The weather was dry and partially cloudy as we set off down the A90 in good spirits.

91

It wasn't long before some of us were little spooked, spotting the same car leapfrogging us as we walked along the road. One of the walkers talked to them, discovering that he was a local farmer checking on the by car. After the hassle approaching Banff, we knew we couldn't be too careful as we passed through Aberdeenshire.

The hike down the main road seemed enjoyably uneventful until we came to a lay-by about two miles outside of Peterhead. We had been told along the way that we should expect lunch in a layby, with soup, coffee/tea and hot rolls. Annoyingly this stretch of the A90 had a number of lay-bys to walk past - making our stomach rumble with anticipation.

Before getting to St. Fergus, we passed what appeared to be a local gas terminal, which had a manned police car parked outside the entrance. Was that typical or did someone get tipped off that we'd be walking down that road? Certainly we had no intention of stopping there.

What a surprise when we came across the next lay-by and spotted a black Land Rover. But also when we spotted one of the Scottish independence movement's best known Twitter celebrities - "Mr. Malky".

Chris Stuart had set out food in the back of his Land Rover including hot burgers, coffee and soup! Thank you again for putting on a wonderful meal. You were such a lifesaver that we wished we could have thanked you more on the day.

To those who don't know, Mr. Malky refers to the name of the owner's previous dog - a perfect way to stay relatively anonymous when not in the right company. Today we met Mr. Malky's owners and their new dog. "Malcolm" was there with both his humans and they all joined us for a twenty minute break to chat about the walk so far.

It was fascinating to hear about the localised political clashes happening in the Aberdeenshire area. The area seems to remain in a holding pattern for the Conservatives, thanks to the combination of an extremely well financed and biased newspaper plus a collection of vocal right wing mouthpieces who manage to get re-elected into government based solely on their party affiliation. Recent history hasn't always treated them well, especially when members of their own party publicly referred to one member as "SNP Gain".

It seemed odd to us - the logic that an independent Scotland wouldn't have to share its oil wealth with the rest of the UK (which in turn would logically make the locals considerably wealthier) was lost here. We do wonder how the UK Government keeps this seemingly simple concept out of the minds of the Aberdeenshire residents.

Surely the local fishing community would also have much more control over how their industry worked with their counterparts in Europe as well, if their demands came from Scotland and not Westminster? Again we're at a loss to understand why, after repeated broken promises and being used as a pawn in trade negotiations, their trust is still extended to the party that only cares about the remaining handful of the richest members in the fishing industry.

The media outlets here must have always been adamantly pro-Conservative - it would otherwise be impossible to be so efficient at adhering to the protective narrative directed from London, instead of Holyrood.

Mr. Malky is a diamond in the rough in these parts, likely because they've experienced a lot more of the world than many folk from Aberdeenshire ever will. They also excel at digging into the details where politicians hoped to gloss over, rewrite or bury the facts.

We all walked together into Peterhead. Mr. Malky popped into the local Boots chemist to purchase some blister plasters for us to use, while Laura stopped outside with local councillor Stephen Calder, who had asked Laura for a shield photo.

We continued walking through Peterhead via the North Road (which Laura amusingly kept correcting herself with the pronunciation - "Peterheeed"). Stopping briefly at the Morrison's supermarket where Wren picked up some supplies and Dean tried unsuccessfully to find a tennis ball to deal with the pains from knots in his back muscles.

Lyndsey was waiting outside looking at a huge stack of fruit on a pallet - all grown in Scotland and packed into cardboard crates, each one covered in union flags. Lyndsey called for an instant photo-shoot of her wearing her Peace Saltire flag while facing the produce. The local shoppers were paying absolutely no attention to us or the obnoxious looking display. If Scottish fruit farmers wanted to alienate their Scottish customers, then they had apparently succeeded admirably. Even in unionist leaning Aberdeenshire, it stood as a shining example of a product marketing failure.

When we made it to the curve in the road on Queen Street, we met up with a large number of Yes Bikers who had stopped to wish us well and some would later help us with security. One of them was Cliff Serbie who was going to be with us in various capacities for most of the rest of the walk. Cliff was apparently the person behind the design of the silhouette logo for the 500 mile badges that were handed out to anyone who walked with us.

After a half hour break we continued on and out of Peterhead. Malcolm the dog and his humans had walked past the marina, completing a respectable four miles with us before deciding to return home. Hugs all around before we said our goodbyes and continued on, crossing the roundabout to rejoin with the A90 heading south. For the longest time, we were blessed with a footpath of some kind. That lasted until the village of Stirling, before reverting to the typical grass verges. Wren, Karl and Andrew Stewart Murray walked ahead, as was their now usual faster pace, while Dean, Jim and Laura took a more leisurely pace at the back, enjoying the unfamiliar sunny weather and admiring the newly deployed windmills that could be seen far out to sea. They look like wee white sticks out in the sea on the horizon, but they are anything but wee.

By the time we got to Longhaven, the walkers returned to a compact group, everyone catching up after taking a break. Laura visited the newsagents and ended up talking to them about our cause and getting more exposure for her shield. Out of the kindness of their hearts, they offered a donation and wished us well.

It wasn't too long before our tired legs reached Hatton, where we reconnected with Dave, Lyndsey and Cliff, as well as Jim Rodden for a meeting with Gillian Martin MSP. Apparently we'd reached the location much later than everyone had planned (sorry!). Due to our late arrival, Gillian didn't really have as much time set aside for us as she'd wanted. We were invited into their family house for some homemade soup, desert and hot drinks while talking politics around their kitchen table.

At times the discussion got heated, where the louder members of the group were trying to talk about the current state of the political situation. To be honest, it often looked like Gillian was starting to feel like she was getting very frustrated, and not getting a word in edgeways. Such is the way when confronted by a group of ardent nationalists. Still, the discussion remained civil and many offers of thanks were handed out for the hospitality.

The quieter members of the group, still in "the zone" were a little frustrated at not being able to get a word in edgeways, but were otherwise extremely grateful for the offer of lunch. Thank you again to Gillian Martin MSP and family for all your hospitality.

Afterwards, we all assembled outside for a photo-shoot before the walking party headed back south on the A90 towards Ellon.

Hiking along the road and grass verge, we noticed that we were running out of daylight again. We made it just shy of Toll of Birness. Surprisingly, all in all we'd already covered 24 miles that day and Ellon was almost another 5 miles ahead. The drivers knew they had to pick us up and relay us to our stop for the night in Ellon.

Here we stayed in a flat of one of Aye Ellon's biggest Yes supporters - best known as "Aye" - Hazel Simpson. The five walkers somehow fitted into the two rooms while Colin and Dave stayed elsewhere.

Before settling down for the night, we were expected to put in an appearance in Peterhead's Yes friendly club, *The Harbour Lights*, where Andrew Stewart Murray had organised for the *Graham Brown Band* to play.

When the walkers entered the room, the entire audience started clapping in appreciation. We didn't know what to say - at least until Laura got her voice back and made a few words of thanks. We were all bought a drink and then were told they were to hold a fund-raiser to help with costs for the walk. Laura helped with this as the rest of us were starting to physically lock-up from all the walking.

Many of the folk who had walked alongside us were also in the audience including Neil Cameron and "Doric" Alan. Neil made an announcement for a whip-round in a hat to raising funds for the walk. Laura, conscious that the donation was additional to their regular food-bank collection, went on stage with her shield to give sincere thanks for their generosity and offered the audience to sign and photograph themselves her HOOP shield. Apparently over a hundred photos were taken holding and signing the shield!

Later, before we left, Melanie Leel (there with her husband Kristopher Leel) handed Laura an extra donation from the younger members. The combined donations amounted to over £250. As the guests of honour, we were truly humbled by the donation of money and receiving a number of their raffle prizes that would typically have supported the local community. Thank you Peterhead for your monetary sacrifice.

After an hour or so there, we were driven back to our sleeping quarters. It was a bit of a cramped night, the lads sleeping in the living room floor in sleeping bags while the lassies shared the bed.

We'd like to say a huge thank you again for the local hospitality. Hazel our host (a vegetarian) had gone to the trouble of getting us food for a hearty Scottish breakfast. As for that night, after getting settled, it didn't take long before we were out like a light.

# DIVERSIONS TO ABERDEEN
## SUNDAY SEPTEMBER 23RD

Sunday started with the smell of Jim's Scottish breakfast being prepared, something we really couldn't appreciate enough as the day unfolded. We had to be out of the house by 8:30am and throw all of our gear in the vehicle as soon as we could.

Today we had a new driver, Colin Mackie, who was an awesome Yes Biker. Dave had to drive his car back to Edinburgh as his wife now needed to use it. So we were to be guided by Colin and Cliff - both of whom owned a box van. Our gear got transferred into the vans, and the remains of our stuff was moved out of Dave's car. Not surprisingly in the usual mad rush - we would later discover that some of our stuff would go missing again for a short while.

We were given general directions and a requirement to make Aberdeen by midday, and set off through a deserted Ellon town centre. We were hoping to avoid the A90 as much as possible today, and that meant we were to walk through Ellon before heading south along a country road. However, something went wrong with our navigation (likely due to the ongoing Aberdeen ring road construction in the area at the time) as it looked like the road we should have taken must have been blocked off. We continued as if nothing happened and ended up walking down the A90 anyway.

It was a dual carriageway at this point, which made no difference to us after all the miles we'd already covered on similar roads. Cliff, trying to catch up with us after we'd left Ellon, had lost us as he didn't have the ability to see our location on GPS. He drove around the area before driving down the A90 in the opposite direction to find us, telling us to stop in the lay-by to chat.

We were heading in the right direction but had to leave the A90 at the earliest opportunity (near Tipperty), and then take the back roads from there. We were directed to head west at Foveran for some reason, so we did and once again fell into the trap of walking long winding and undulating country roads that looked much more level and straight on a map.

Whilst walking, Dean had been monitoring our location and distance covered with a GPS app on his phone. When Cliff stopped by to check on the walkers, Dean indicated to Cliff that our diversion had made us an hour off our target of making downtown Aberdeen by midday. The walkers had no idea what the point of the noon deadline was, but it made no difference. It wasn't that the walkers hadn't covered the distance, the problem was simply that their unplanned diversion had taken them too far off track to make the firm time commitment.

Cliff drove to meet up with Colin, our other driver and discussed what they could do. Even though we were in the middle of nowhere, the walkers couldn't be seen getting in and out of a van, or folk would talk. It would be a bad look if we looked like we'd not been walking at all. How would we be able to prove it when we'd been walking along mostly deserted Sunday morning roads? In the end, both vehicles picked up everyone and dropped us off a few miles down the road on the B999. We were now back on track and on the right road, having already covered the equivalent number of miles and heading into Aberdeen on the main road.

A little after walking through Mundurno, we met up with Nicholas again, ready to march into town with his now familiar kilt and saltire flag outfit. The weather stayed sunny and the special flag designed by "Brave" was standing out for all the busy traffic to boldly see.

We cut through the industrial estate at Cloverhill and then zigzagged through to the Parkway, taking the well worn footpaths down the A956 into Aberdeen. We had a local Yes supporter on Rollerblades who joined us for the rest of the trek into the city centre, as we all hiked down the straight path of Ellon Road.

As we approached the city centre, by St. Andrews Cathedral, a number of Yessers came to meet us and tell us it wasn't far for us to go! "The Aberdeen Piper" lead the walkers towards Castlegate. Once we had crossed the road, we could see in the distance a large gathering of people there for us.

Aberdeen has two Yes groups. Yes Aberdeen 2 and the Aberdeen Independence Movement (AIM). They had gone all-out for us today, with a paper banner signed by many of their supporters and we were joined by like minded folk making speeches. Laura, Nicholas and Wren all contributed to the speeches too, to grand applause. We were completely moved, some to tears.

The *Aberdeen Press and Journal* newspaper

surprisingly said we were "welcomed by a crowd of hundreds"! Some of the local SNP councillors were also there to meet us. Afterwards, AIM kept the banner for the time being so that everyone who hadn't signed it, could do so. Jim would later receive it, after the walk was completed.

The same *Press and Journal* website posted an article "Watch as hundreds flock to Aberdeen Indyref2 rally" including video of our arrival into Castlegate square connecting us to the Yes groups push for a new independence referendum.

Yes Aberdeen 2 co-chair Rory Macpherson said: "The walkers are bringing the independence movement to all the far-flung communities in Scotland. And it was great to see so many folk come out. They passed through Fraserburgh and I heard some people there say it was the first time they had something like this near them in decades". This was exactly what the 500 mile walkers wanted to hear.

Paul Anderson, a local student activist said: "We want our children to grow up in a Scotland with a safe and secure environment." We could not agree more.

Fiona Robertson gave a rousing speech, comparing Scotland to the rest of the UK, saying: "We already are doing better. Imagine what we could do with the full range of financial powers we could have."

The atmosphere was electric and not dissimilar to the All Under One Banner marches that would later come to Aberdeen.

Local SNP councillors had put on lunch for all of us at the La Lombarda Restaurant that was located on the corner of the square by the Mercat Cross. We were worn out after the cross country hiking in the sun, so took the opportunity to sit and eat. We'd like to thank everyone who helped pay the bill before we left.

On Twitter, Fiona Robertson said "Fantastic afternoon at the @500Miles4Indy rally - music, singing, speeches and a lot of smiles in the sunshine. Great to have the [chance] to talk about the kind of Scotland we're trying to build - one where everyone is part of our society however they're able. #500Miles".

Laura had a surprise, two very good friends Eleanor Bennett of Yes Kirkcaldy and Pam had driven up to surprise us, donating a bottle of Jura whisky, appropriately called Journey, to wish us luck and speed us on our way.

A Scottish Rugby saltire onesie had been offered for luck in honour of the Lothian MSP Margo MacDonald who had passed away in the run up to the 2014 independence referendum. The onesie was bought for the summer 2014 by the friends of Margo MacDonald for wearing overnight on the night of the referendum count to sleep on Arthur's Seat. Even though Margo wasn't there for the night, Elenor and friends still climbed Holyrood and raised a glass to Margo. Elenor wanted Laura to carry the onesie as a symbolic symbol showing that Margo had walked with us and to keep warm during the colder nights.

The walkers were sad to have to leave Aberdeen so promptly, but our daily hike was only half done. Jim would later realise he'd forgotten his phone at the restaurant.

For the second half of our walk, we were joined by two local NHS nurses who had decided to join us to walk from Aberdeen to our ending point. It was their first day off in over a month! Thank you both for making the sacrifice of your time to join us - we all appreciated it.

Darline and her husband also joined us as we hiked along Union Street. The sky threatened us with a little rain, fortunately it was short-lived. We all stopped for photographs outside Ross Thompson MP's office with Nicholas holding his iPad up with a heart symbol for use on his social media account.

We carried on towards Bridge of Dee, and somehow managed to walk the longest way around a roundabout while trying to determine how best to cross the River Dee. Eventually we got there and continued up towards Tollohill Wood. It was fortunate that we had received directions from local Yes Biker, Craig McKenzie for getting across to Portlethen.

It was after hiking up the hill, chatting with our two local walkers and getting photographs of the Aberdeen skyline behind us, that we finally reached the summit and an unmapped section of the new Aberdeen bypass (known as the "Aberdeen Western Peripheral Route").

There was a recently completed bridge that we had to walk over. The still unopened road below looked flawless from above. The yellowing sunlight on the horizon also showed us that there was probably only an hour of daylight left to walk. Dean stopped for photographs while the rest of the party carried on.

We continued through country roads, taking a turn at Badentoy and down Cookston Road. We took a right turn here, to the car park at the local supermarket. This was the end point for our hiking today having covered about 21 miles.

By the time we'd got to the supermarket, most of the smaller shops were already closed. Some of the walkers stocked up on pain killers and plasters in Asda while they had the chance.

Dean finally found something to relieve his back pain - a tennis ball sized toy that was transparent with a flashing light in it. He didn't care for the design, only that it would help tame the knots in his back muscles.

In the car park, Eleanor and Pam who we'd met at lunch time were waiting in the car park when we arrived to offer our two additional walkers a ride back to Aberdeen. Thanks again to all of you for your support.

Colin drove the 500miler's to the *Aberdeen Northern Hotel* in his van. Yes Biker "Spyro" had joined Colin for the trip.

Darren Murray was a Yes Biker and a manager at the hotel. We later discovered that Darren, Spyro and a third Yes Biker, Craig Mackenzie, had paid out of pocket for our stay for the night. Not discovering this until later, we were all gob-smacked from their generosity.

Jim realised he'd misplaced his phone somewhere, so he phoned the restaurant we'd stopped in at lunchtime. They had already handed it into the police. So now Jim had to contact the Aberdeen police, and with Laura who hadn't had a drink yet, drove Darren's car to the police station with Spyro. At the police station, Jim was handed his phone back without any questions asked.

The rest of us, waiting in the lobby talked, had photographs with our supporters and took the opportunity to finally relax with a drink. Waiting for the phone search party to return before grabbing dinner.

We were all told to be ready to leave at 8am and that we had to grab a breakfast which started at 7am.

The team split up into two rooms and most took the first opportunity to fix their feet for the day ahead. It was truly heavenly - the showers were wonderful. The guys room had a bath tub so Dean took the opportunity to relax his back muscles and soak his feet in the steaming hot water.

After all our camping adventures, the hotel beds were so comfy that most were out like a light, a respite before discovering who snored the worst. Colin stuck with Dave in the only bed left that night, later claiming Dave's snoring was "like a elephant with air horns"!

# £100 & A FRIED MARS BAR
## MONDAY SEPTEMBER 24TH

Monday morning didn't start out well.
The two rooms where the walkers had slept were split between Laura, Wren and Karl in one family room and Dave, Colin, Dean and Jim in the other. The guys in Dave's room were all up and ready to eat breakfast at 7am, to be ready to drive back to Portlethen at 8am. Karl and Wren were late getting ready, hadn't had breakfast yet and Dave was starting to look like he was going to "blow a fuse" from the lack of communication.

After eating a full Scottish breakfast, Dean and Jim were eager and ready to walk and so offered to go earlier. That way someone could make the meet up point at Stonehaven by the expected arrival time of 11am. Any further delay would have meant that folk waiting for us would likely have left already - again.

Dave begrudgingly drove the first two walkers to the starting point in the middle of Portlethen, before driving back to pickup the rest of the team. Wren was livid that Jim and Dean had left without them, claiming to be ready to go by a quarter past eight. Since Wren and Karl had already lost a few miles covered from previous mornings sleeping in, they refused to join Jim and Dean, wanting instead to walk the whole distance starting from the same point in Portlethen.

The hike along the road to Stonehaven was mostly on a footpath, until it unceremoniously ended in the middle of nowhere for absolutely no particular reason. It then became a thin dirt cycle track. The walkers found it easier to hike on the cut grass instead. The scenic views along the coast road were wonderful and we didn't have to walk on the road itself for very long at all. Jim and Dean made it into Stonehaven at the expected time, to be met by various members of the local Stonehaven and Mearns SNP and Yes community at various points down the brae into town.

Along the northern point of the main street is a community centre and swimming baths with a park outside. We were lead to this park. Here the local community cafe had supplied us with bowls of soup, sandwiches and coffee. We'd like to thank Isla and Jean Duncan (two of Stonehaven's biggest Yes supporters) for the terrific meal they put on for all of us.

The Stonehaven supporters were a little unhappy that the walkers had split up into two groups, but since half the crowd had to leave to do other things, we were at least happy to have part of the team make it on time.

Dean took the time to have a long chat with Bill Emilie, a true legend and long standing activist for independence. Bill's friends pointed out that his cottage can always be found proudly flying a saltire.

Carole was here playing with her dog Barry, who was partially blind. We were to meet again later in the day. The weather improved as the morning progressed, becoming a very pleasant sunny day.

111

The second half of the walkers arrived almost an hour later, none too happy looking, but held off having an argument about it. At least now the team was all in one place, and we could continue from here. Unfortunately the long delay would cost us in distance covered for that day.

Laura had previously met with many of the Stonehaven Yes members in June. Here she met with the local councillor Christine Mann who donated two envelopes with £100 (£50 each from Stonehaven and Mearns Yes and the local SNP group) towards the 500miles walk. Fiona McCarron Morrison and Karen Emilie met with Laura and offered an additional envelope with a donation. Thank you everyone.

We all met up with local Yes members including the Twitter Yes supporter, Callum McSwan, more commonly known with his social media handle, "The Black Saltire". Nicholas and Laura took the time to walk down to the beach with Bill Emilie and take more photographs.

Around midday, we re-gathered and started a mini-parade with lots of flags flying, along the main street. Here the locals were telling us everything they could about their local community. Their local pride and desire for independence was admirable. Locals who joined us included Harry and Eileen Bickerstaff, Christine Mann, Alison and Robin Barclay and Glen Brown.

Nicholas had popped into the local fish and chip shop, The Bay Fish & Chips, made famous for their claim to invent the deep fried Mars bars. The rest of us were a little short on realising that this was where it originated, and most of us passed up trying it so soon after lunch. With flags waving and everyone smiling, the local community seemed fine with us making a bit of a fuss parading through town. We kept walking, turning up the brae on the south side of town which was road that closely followed the coast line. Towards the peak, we had a wee break before saying our farewells to some of the locals. The walkers continued on with a few of the more experienced local hikers.

Robin and Alison Barclay lead the rest of us as the local expert walkers to Dunnottar Castle. Here we took a brief break to gather everyone together and take photographs. The owners of the castle had no issues with the group of 500 mile walkers visiting and getting group photographs.

The next section was back to the winding and hilly sections of back roads. Had we walked down the A92, we would have easily made it to our destination, but that route was not realistic for a group of pedestrians. We hiked the long and winding back roads, passing near Crawton, Catterline and Kinneff. Here we took a well needed snack break, putting our feet up and chatting with Robin and Alison, our expert walkers that day. We reluctantly got back on our tired and worn feet, continuing along the country roads into Inverbervie.

In Inverbervie we were in for an unexpected shock. First we were greeted by Aileen Grosset and her daughter who were determined to give £100 to the 500mile walkers. Laura, who had become our default secretary, keeping notes of all the donations for legal purposes, received the money that had just been withdrawn from a local cash-point. Laura thought that the very generous donation was more than Aileen should have offered. Aileen was determined to offer the donation without accepting anything less. Laura was almost reduced to tears and the rest of the team were visibly shocked. Thank you so much Aileen.

Dean was starting to struggle with blisters, looking for any kind of relief from the local chemist. Wren and Karl also visited the local shops for supplies. Nicholas took the opportunity to record a video message with Robin Barclay, which showed off Robin's impressive poetic talents. How Robin hiked this entire way while carrying a huge flagpole and flag is anyone's guess. The main walkers were truly exhausted.

We'd been expected to get at least half of the rest of the way to Laurencekirk on foot, but the quickly setting sun and our earlier delays earlier made it unrealistic. The winding rural roads into Laurencekirk would have taken us three more hours to cover the remaining 10 miles. We had already covered over 20 miles that day. The sunny weather in the afternoon was a pleasant change, but it also added to our exhaustion from the drawn out walk.

We were scheduled to stop at the steps to the Laurencekirk school for a photo opportunity with the Yes/SNP community from Lawrencekirk and Stonehaven Mearns. This meant we'd need to be there before the sun set. With a collective sigh of relief, we all jumped in the back of the support van.

In Laurencekirk we had an amusing conundrum as there were two schools. Strangely no one in our group knew which school we were expected to go to. We later discovered that nobody had thought about the primary school hidden away at the polar opposite end of town. Eventually after some walking and driving back and forth along the main street looking for a familiar face, we made it to the right location for 7 o'clock.

Our photo shoot was done on the steps, under the

waning rays of daylight, where we joined by many of the local Yes/SNP supporters. We were greeted with an offer of a night staying in Carole Wise's house, whom we'd met earlier at our lunchtime stop in Stonehaven. She had prepared for us all a most delicious slow cooked chilli and rice dinner. We all had a great time chatting, and talking about the events so far, many of us packed in around Carole's kitchen. The chilli truly hit the spot.

After getting ready, showering and the like, rooms were allocated for the walkers. Dean had been relegated to the living room due to his snoring! Dave had stopped in the living room to plug in his phone to put it on charge, while resting his head on Dean's duffel bag. In under a minute, Dave was unconscious and likely wasn't going to move again until the following morning. Fortunately Dean could get by without the use of anything in the bag, and he slept on the hardwood floor in his sleeping bag.

Laura settled in the downstairs front room opposite Dean and Dave, where she worked into the evening on her laptop. Before sleeping, Carole had run Laura a bath with Epsom Salts, which she later shared was heavenly.

Everyone else slept upstairs with the luxury of proper beds. Unsurprisingly, it didn't take long before just about everyone was out like a light.

# BLETHERING
## TUESDAY SEPTEMBER 25TH

After yesterday's horrific start, today started off more akin to a military operation. Everyone up at the right time, out the door and on our way after saying our thanks to Carole for her terrific hospitality.

The main walkers walked south-west along the High Street through Laurencekirk. Two of them popped to the primary school car park to see if anyone was up for walking with us (sadly no) before everyone continued on towards the A90. With only a grass verge to use (thanks to the shear amount of traffic), this was going to be another tough slog. We persevered on. After a mile or so along the way, we picked up two Yes supporters who told us they had followed our trails online.

Here Brechin resident Paul Wright and his good friend James Gill joined us for what was to become a very long day indeed. After a few miles walking alongside the A90, we were flagged down to eastern exit near North Water Bridge. The five miles we'd walked down the grass verge had been brutal on our feet and it wasn't going to get any easier. We took a little while to recuperate alongside the exit road, while a local supporter had stopped to provide us with some well appreciated bites to eat and a hot drink from their SUV.

This was probably the first time we'd actually walked almost the entire time on grass verges, and we'll all tell you this makes walking long distances between towns near impossible. Thanks to the uneven ground full of ruts, potholes and lots of old rubbish, we discovered first hand how you end up with blisters. Being lead a different way was crucial as we'd realistically only make it another 7 miles if we had continued along the A90.

A short distance away at the Stracathro services on the A90, Dave and Laura had stopped to meet Nicholas and grab food while tracking the walkers. It was here that Laura met Ian Dixon (who Laura hadn't seen since Catalonia, when he was there with other councillors including Julie Bell - an old friend of Jim) and picked up a hot water bottle for Wren with a picture of a unicorn.

We took a small road, which started to back track before heading for Templewood and the connection to the B966. This road lead us to Brechin and it had a footpath the entire way! The B966 becomes Trinity Road and leads directly into the heart of town.

A right turn onto Swan Street and we were greeted by the enthusiastic crowd at the Brechin Blether~In, the name of their pro-independence hub that was intentionally meant to be open to everyone for a chat, without being unrelentingly "Yes". The shop was split in two parts, with an office like area downstairs and an area set out with tables and chairs around it upstairs. The local supporters had gone all-out and made a huge buffet (collectively supplied by many local supporters) that was a truly unexpected surprise. We were truly famished, appreciating every bite. It felt so kind and welcoming, much like being at home.

Some of the names we managed to note down included Lyn Smith, Ruth Watson, Jenny Matchett and Angus councillor Julie Bell.

Sadly we had to cut our visit shorter than we would have liked. We had to leave and walk to the other Blether~In before the day was over! Paul Wright, who was walking with us that day, asked if anyone was going to do any artwork to show our walking route across Scotland. The route we were walking reflected the form of a number 2. Strangely most of us hadn't even noticed, but the cross from Skye over the Highlands and down the coast and inwards heading for Stirling and Glasgow before crossing to Edinburgh, certainly resembled the number. We were not actually told much about the planning phase, but presume this was intentional to reflect Indyref 2.

Shortly after getting back on our feet and leaving Brechin, we came to Netherton. This was our half way point and home of the Davidson family - better known as the Scottish motorcycle pioneer - the Davidson of Harley-Davidson fame. None of us had any idea that Davidson was born in Scotland. Waiting by the gate in front of the Davidson house, the walkers met up with Mike Sinclair who has a Facebook page that shares information about "The Davidson Legacy". Mike called ahead to Paul Duncan who would meet with us shortly when we reached the nearby Pictish Stones.

Nicholas, in awe of the unexpected Davidson discovery, took the opportunity to take plenty of photos with the Harley-Davidson logo on the flag behind him.

While posting images online, Nicholas discovered that the Indy Poet, Paul Colvin had posted another poem for the 500 mile walkers, this time titled #500miles:

#500miles    © Paul Colvin.

Aye! They're battered, blistered, bruised with cuts upon their feet,
But they're full of vigour wrapped in hope where each step erodes defeat,
They are walking for awareness for our Independent cause
And in every place they come to, they are welcomed with applause.

Battling through the elements that saps their passion's powers,
They garner strength from our support, as we, from them, get ours
For they are bolstered by a great belief that spurs them on inside
And that belief is Independence and they know we're by their side.

Their inner strength, that eager will, is forged within a heart
That stands against a Union that wants our country ripped apart
But love and pain unites these hearts to give them strength to fight,
To capture steely Scots' resolve and claim our Sovereign rights.

They will let them know they're sovereign and let them know they're not alone

And that Scots will choose their future, where our choices are our own,
And these raggle taggle gypsies with their freedom bell in hand
Walk with a passion in their hearts some will never understand

There's a pride that's beamed across this land, inspiring all who see
Scotland's sons and daughters who are friends to you and me,
They've seen the sights and heard the sounds and smelt our sweetest air,
They've paved the way for all of us, they're the storm we all will share.

Here, there are no leaders and though they may be few
They walk for me and those who can't, for freedom and for you
Yet already they're victorious though only half their miles they've trekked
So I salute these marchers proudly, they've more than earned our respect.

Worn down, they may be but for them, this walk, this quest
Is not for glorious egos or for bright medals pinned on chests
We should honour them as they've honoured us, every single name
They are our heroes, heroines and for that, have our acclaim.

Dave read it aloud from his phone, and we were all left awestruck. The fact that we'd not been able to spend much time on social media meant that we were completely unaware of the posts everyone was sharing describing their experiences and spotting us traversing across Scotland.

We continued further up the hill to get to Aberlemno, while noticing that the noticeably colder cross winds had really started to blow. Three of the Pictish Stones straddle the side of the road. A few of us decided to take the time to study them and get photographs alongside. Laura, Dave, Dean and Colin took the time to talk to Paul Duncan, a local resident and hall committee member, while standing in front of the large replica battle stone made specially for the location by Edinburgh sculptor Andrew McFetters.

While standing by one of the pictish stones (the one with the serpent), we were met by Kenny Braes and Neil Cameron again.

Kenny took a photograph of Neil holding his Cameron flag with Laura and Dean. He'd used Neil's phone to take the photograph and Neil later used that image in his first ever tweet. Kenny is one of the Angus councillors who lived nearby and had met us earlier at Brechin's Blether~In. Laura recalled Kenny saying to Neil, "I love the 500 miles so much that I can't leave them alone" - not surprising that we'd meet again later shortly in Tealing!

Neil had made a special trip to stop by and give Laura a replica claymore sword for her to use at the Edinburgh march. He tweeted "Well done guys. You crossed a huge milestone today at the half way point having walked 250 miles of #500miles march for

Independence. Great to catch up with you all for a short time", before he had to leave to go to work.

Since the majority of the walking party had continued on ahead, the three of us didn't have a chance to really take in the gravity of the history in this area. We did however take the opportunity to take a break, give a donation and a huge thanks, before continuing on.

Dean and Laura were now far behind the rest of the walkers, while Dave continued on in the support vehicle, alternating between the two groups. The gusty wind was getting colder and Laura was having a difficult time keeping up. Dean stuck with her, albeit trying to push ahead to catch up with the others. After taking a corner, and having a long view ahead, Dean realised that the rest of the team must have been at least a half mile or more in front, so continued on at a less strenuous pace down the B9134.

The team in front had no idea what had happened to Dean and Laura, but it was familiar territory to Jim, so they continued on to their destination. In Lunanhead, Jim met up with Bill Duff who said "I support Scottish Independence because I believe Scotland should run its own affairs. We are an ancient country and are more than capable of making better decisions for our people that a parliament in London."

By the time Dean and Laura had made it 2½ miles down the road to "Pitscandly", they came across Paul Wright, leaning against a gate. Paul had hit the point where he couldn't walk anymore and was waiting for the next bus home. Pitscandly is located about 1½ miles outside Forfar and is effectively a field with a road through it. Dean called Dave in the support vehicle, mentioned that they should come and pick up Paul. While the weather was dry, the harsh wind wasn't remotely helpful. Taking Paul to the Blether-In in Forfar for warmth and a bite to eat was what Paul appeared to need now, more than anything else. Laura and Dean kept on walking, while Dave and Colin came back to pickup Paul in the support van.

The team reconnected at before walking into Forfar. A number of local supporters had come to meet up with all the walkers at this point. Here we met up again with Nicholas and a number of the gang we'd made friends with at the Brechin Blether~In earlier that day. We paraded into town. More and more people joined us and walk alongside, until we met a large congregation of people in the centre of town.

Of course, not everything went to plan, we did encounter an older woman amongst the crowd in Forfar who was quite obviously not pro-indy. They tried to look like a supporter, then throw out their greasy words of negativity. She was respectfully ignored - this wasn't the place nor the time for giving the poor soul an audience for spouting unionist propaganda. We were all exhausted after walking another 25 miles. We all needed a break, not an argument.

We were lead by a crowd of supporters through Forfar's High Street to their Blether-In site. This was already full of people, including Colin (who had taken over control of the computer, playing appropriately themed music videos found on the Internet).

In preparation for our arrival, Margaret Pollock had made a special rectangular cake, covered in white frosting and the top displayed the image we had taken on our first night in Skye - the one where we light painted "I would walk #500miles" across it. For Dean who took the photo (and permitting everyone pro-Indy to use the image for free) it came as a bit of a pleasant

126

shock. Candles were lit and Jim and Laura, who were still able to stand on their feet, blew out the candles.

The Forfar Yes group had put on sandwiches, tea and coffee. A piece of the 500 miles themed cake topped that all off, but not before being allocated into groups for a place to stay for the night. We spent a relaxing hour there having a good chat with everyone, singing along to the music that Colin was discovering. We all celebrated making it the whole day starting from Laurencekirk and visiting both Blether-In's. A few of us even dared to take off our boots for a wee rest. We weren't going anywhere soon.

Kenny Braes joined us again, together with Ian Dickson and Julie Bell who offered us a foot spa that would later become a necessity. Other names and faces we remember included Isabelle Davies, Juliette O'Keeffe, Ruth Watson (behind "Keep Scotland the Brand", which was started right here) and Margaret Pollock.

Dean stayed with Jim at his home in nearby Kirriemuir, driven there by Ruth Watson. Laura, Wren and Karl stayed at Margaret Pollock's home nearby.

Many in the movement know Margaret Pollock as a staunch Yes supporter and long standing SNP member. She had generously set out her house ready for the walkers and set them up with a wonderful breakfast the next morning.

# BLISTERING
## WEDNESDAY SEPTEMBER 26TH

NÍL AON TÓIN TINN MAR DO THÓIN TINN FÉIN.

At 8am the walkers regrouped in the car park, located behind Forfar's High Street. Everyone transferred their belongings into Colin's van. Today we had eight eager supporters from Forfar, Yes Kirrie and beyond, joining us for our long days hike towards Dundee.

The bone chilling wind had died down today, and it looked like another relatively dry day was ahead of us. We walked out of Forfar along Dundee Road.

Just after we left the edge of town (before Dundee Road ran into the A90) we took the farm track leading us westwards. We were hoping this would be a more appropriate way to get to Tealing (which happens to be alongside the A90) without hiking for miles along the treacherous roadside.

While we walked through the countryside, there were no trails, roads, tracks or anything that we could see that would lead us in a direction that would bring us to Inveraldie. We saw some wonderful scenery, talked with local farmers (including one driving past in his tractor) before asking the local bin-lorry drivers for guidance.

The best we could find, took us at least a mile further

west than we wanted to be. We all hiked through Kincaldrum and Charleston before finding a route south and east that would bring the group to the A90 again. The hike was most certainly not flat and the roads twisting and turning. By Charleston, Dean's blistered feet were demanding a break and he was made to jump in the back of the vehicle, to be driven ahead to Inveraldie for much needed pain relief.

Laura also took the opportunity to jump into the van, as she had arranged a live mobile phone interview with Johanna Ross from Sputnik News UK that morning.

While on the interview with Sputnik News, Laura was asked if now was the "time for the SNP to call Indyref2?". Of course her answer was "Yes". Sputnik immediately ran an article "Message to the SNP: it's time for you to call IndyRef2", mentioning that we were expecting to meet hundreds of people in Dundee.

The remaining team of walkers plodded on, only to get to the A90 and thought they had found a short-cut for hiking in Tealing. Sadly they discovered it didn't go where they wanted to, so backtracked to the A90 and continued walking down the grass verge again. Eventually everyone made it to Inveraldie.

The community centre in Inveraldie was the home of Yes Monifieth. Here, Dean had discovered the real benefit of foot baths - devices that were commonly gifted years ago and now gathering dust in most people's closets and garages (including Dean's)! When used with enough Epsom salts, hot water and time, they can be heavenly. Earlier, Dean's feet didn't look like they'd be going anywhere for the rest of that day. After soaking in Epsom salts, topped up with hot water for an hour, he was finally able to put his socks and hiking boots back on. When Wren later walked into the community centre, Dean passed on the use of the foot bath, to help her with the nagging blisters on her feet.

Yes Monifieth had put on a wonderful selection of sandwiches, snack food and (most importantly) tablet. What we didn't know until someone blurted, was that the tablet was made by a number of Yes Monifieth members. They all wanted to know who's tablet was rated the best by the walkers. We can only say that it was all wonderful tasting. We were so grateful for all the terrific food, great company and all the kind hearted assistance on our hike that day.

None of the walkers wanted to leave that community centre, especially after the harsh hike to get there. Lots of pictures and selfies were taken. We'd all like to say a thank you to everyone joining us there, especially Marlene McBay and Jean Lee.

Reluctantly, the 500 mile walkers got ready to continue on. James Gill had surprised us, joining again to walk alongside us into Dundee. Just as we were leaving we noticed the vinyl sign hung up on the trees alongside the A90. It said "Toot for Indy" by Yes Monifieth. Based on how many vehicles were honking their horns, it was doing a great job.

Leaving Inveraldie for Dundee required walking down the dual carriageway of the A90. This meant we had to hike nearly one and a half miles down the grass verge. There were no pedestrian friendly options until we came across the first road bridge, with a bus stop connected to it with concrete steps. We all happily walked up the steps, crossed the bridge and hiked down that road instead.

Curving down Emmock Road, we met up with two

police officers in their vehicle that wanted to talk to us. Apparently someone had called in that we were walking down the verge of the A90. Did someone presume we were doing something illegal or did a disgruntled driver want to terminate our 500 mile walk before getting to Dundee? Either way, we had obviously succeeded in attracting wanted attention to our walk.

The officers were there waiting for us, following through on the call. We all approached their car calmly. As expected they said we were doing nothing wrong. Having already been told our rights in Skye, the officers reminded us that it was perfectly legal to walk down any road, with exceptions for motorways or when posted "no pedestrians" for our own safely. We said our thanks and they wished us well on our walk. To the driver who called in the 500 Mile walkers to the police from Dundee, and to the kind police officers themselves - thank you so much for caring about our well-being.

Emmock Road turns a corner and becomes the road the runs alongside the A90, which shortly reintroduces the seemingly foreign concept of a footpath! At Fintry street, we were surprised to be met by a piper. Jimmy Black, the former housing convener for Dundee, was piping for our arrival into the "Yes city". Nicholas was also patiently standing alongside him waving his special saltire flag and happy to be able to join us again.

The expanding walking team continued walking alongside the main road before crossing over the A90 on the footbridge and into the Caird Park area of Dundee (in order to avoid the sections road that were not pedestrian friendly). We were taking a short cut through the side of the golf course, that lead us to Kingsway. Fortunately Dave was walking with us at that point and he knew the best route to take. Walking west, we looped around the roundabout and headed south, across two roundabouts before taking various roads that lead us down the hill into the heart of Dundee, past Desperate Dan and into the City Square where we were met again by a piper.

This was where we expected to meet up with the Yes Dundee crowd. But we appeared to hit on the beginning of an annoying planning oversight. There were a handful of locals from the Dundee area waiting there including "Wee Annie". We had expected a much more significant number to meet us. We were met by local "Jock McAngus" who also goes by the nickname "Heretic Jock". They told us that they were expecting us to arrive the following day. We were understandably crestfallen at hearing this and wondered what had occurred.

Apparently there was some confusion due to the fact that the publicly shared information about the route indicated the starting point for each day and little mention of the route to the end. It didn't help that the list of locations we were visiting made no mention of Dundee - we were expected to finish in Inchture that day. Apparently the Yes Dundee group were never told a day and time when we were expected to arrive. We can only say we were extremely sorry to have missed the chance to meet-up with everyone, knowing how important it was to everyone.

After waiting in Dundee's City Square for a short while, most of us exited down the stairs and headed towards Dundee's new V&A building. The builders had just recently removed the construction barriers, to reveal a beautiful facade. We walked as far as the car park next to the discovery centre and took a break.

Laura had stayed back in Dundee's City Square because she had been met by four of the Dundee council group, recognising that she was wearing a 500 miles vest. They all wanted to chat and get a photograph with the shield. Laura then caught up with the other walkers at the V&A.

The team had covered about 24 miles that day and looking at the map of Scotland, had walked around the whole peninsular that surrounds the Cairngorns. This mental image was starting to become hard to get our head around. How did we accomplish that seemingly impossible feat?

After a break and talking to some tourists interested in our hike, we could see the evening was starting to draw in. We were told to jump into the back of the van where we were taken to a place to stay for the night in Inchture.

We were under the impression that we'd be staying somewhere akin to a hostel or such. Dave had made some arrangements with one of the local Yes supporters who had a business there.

When the group arrived, Dave quickly realised that this didn't look like what he was expecting. The property was deserted with no sign of anyone else. It appeared like we were meant to camp out on the lawn next to the building. While we appreciated the gesture (and presume that was the intent), after all that we'd been through, none of us were satisfied with that option.

This called for 'plan B'. Jim's daughter and family lived in Broughty Ferry - located on the opposite side of Dundee. Jim was happy to contact them to see if that was an option. After a quick phone call, we were whisked off to our home-from-home for the night, in the wonderful company of Elaine and Chris, and their warm and welcoming house.

Our impromptu visit meant a call for local fish 'n' chips was in order. Chris was so considerate to share a dram of whisky with us too. Thank you to you both for putting us all up at such short notice. And thank you for the excellent whisky! Slàinte mhath.

# WELCOME TO PERTH
## THURSDAY SEPTEMBER 27TH

Inchture had always been the planned starting location for that day's hike. The distance on roads that straddle the River Tay from Dundee to Inchture would have added a couple of additional hours to our hike - time that we were told we didn't have.

After giving thanks to Elaine and Chris, and a quick stop by a local newsagents to pickup a copy of The National, we were transported in the van across Dundee to Inchture. We had been left with basic directions to "follow this road which would take us towards St. Madoes", hoping to catch up with us again before reaching the A90. Dave and Colin had to drive ahead to determine how walkers could get from the road to the walking path/cycle track on the A90 since it wasn't clear on any maps we had.

The walkers were not made aware of anyone joining us during that day's hike. Jim, Dean, Wren, Karl and Laura proceeded on foot, walking through the village to the roundabout before heading south-east on a very long straight road.

It was along this road that the walkers quickly came

across a huge potato warehouse, realising that all the tractors we had seen over the last few days (all pulling large wooden crates) were likely on their way to this central warehouse. Passing by the open entryway, we could see there were hundreds if not thousands of these crates stacked high and deep. The smell of fresh potatoes was strangely intense and continued drifting down the road we were walking along for some time.

This made us wonder. Most potatoes sold in grocery stores across Scotland have a union flag on the bag - even those sold by Scottish brands such as Bartlets.

Could this be the storage and distribution point for all the potatoes we eat everyday across the country? It turns out this is one of them. We were later told that there are a few more warehouses, one of which is in the Scottish Borders. We're just as mystified as anyone, why Scottish potatoes are always marketed as British.

We continued down the straight road, annoyed by the high cross winds that made it a very cold journey. Dean happened to come across a damaged St. Christopher pendant on the side of the road, and stopped to pick it up. Did we now have the patron saint of travellers behind us? We would soon find out.

After walking a good distance pounded by heavy cross winds, we were grateful that the road took a sharp turn and the wind was no longer any trouble. We walked through Grange, and onwards to Errol.

In Errol, we came across two people who were surprised to see us passing through their village and wished us well, taking selfie photographs with us. Errol was a pleasant little village, and we took an unscheduled snack break at the top of High Street on the corner onto St. Madoes Road. Dave and Colin had planned on us walking further up the same road (that then lead north west to the A90) and had stopped at the same spot, patiently waiting for us. After they returned to our resting spot, we said it made more sense to walk directly to St. Madoes on a more direct road heading west. So that became the revised plan.

In St. Madoes, Wren managed to find a place to take a toilet break at the doctors, while the rest of us sat alongside the road. Dave and Colin were waiting for us at the edge of the village to tell us what our next steps were. The next section required us to walk from St. Madoes turn-off on the A90, to take the next exit. We would be using a bicycle track/footpath that was built alongside the road.

Dave, Colin and Laura left to visit The Chestnut Tree for a bite to eat and a toilet break. Dave said his spinach soup was the best he'd ever had. On paying for the meals, Fleur the owner, offered their coffees for free. The regular customers of The Chestnut Tree cafe seemed, understandably, of a different political persuasion. Even so, everyone was extremely welcoming. The owners, in deep admiration for the endurance of the 500miles walkers, wanted a photograph with Laura's shield, taking badges and mutual thanks were exchanged.

Using social media to contact the local Yes movement, Laura received a message with an offer for our accommodation for that night. It took her less than 30 minutes to get a definitive answer.

The walkers hiked past the longest section of poly-tunnels any of us had seen before. Working on the tunnels were a number of European workers who were quite interested to see us and we passed them a few of the 500 miles walk badges we'd been handing out along the way. We hope for the local farming communities sake, that Brexit doesn't result in the loss of these huge sources of Scottish grown fruit. That in itself would result in a huge knock on effect to Dundee's famous jam and marmalade businesses.

Just before getting to turn off at Kinfauns Junction, the weather turned and we were given a short sharp drenching. It was here that Nicholas rejoined us with his flag and iPad. He had also bought a brand new mobile phone that had a much better camera to his old iPhone. We proceeded to ignore the rain while Nicolas tested the waterproofing of his gadgets.

Here we got a little confused with our instructions, but followed the road north east, to the first major turn which went through Kinfauns and came out on the ridge of Kinnoull Hill Woodland Park. Fortunately they hadn't mentioned the extremely steep hill walk to get here beforehand. The rain started to let up and we made it to the park at the top and wondered if we were expected to wait there or continue.

At the top of the brae, we met up again with Colin and Dave in the van. The clear view to the south west was simply stunning. We took a brief break to resupply. Laura got out of the van and rejoined us to complete the rest of the walk into Perth.

Stopping at the Jubilee car park, Karl and Wren thought maybe the party we were expecting to meet was up the track - so we all hiked up a half mile only to find nothing! Returning we finally made contact with our drivers and kept on walking towards Perth.

Arriving at the first signs of houses, we made a turn onto Corsie Hill Road to another turn off/park where a bunch of Yes supporters were there waiting for us to arrive. It was here that we were told we were to start a mini-parade down Hatton Road and Bowerswell Road to the A85 road that lead over the West Bridge in Perth.

To be fair, we'd been a little beaten up by the hill and the rain shower, and appreciated the slow hike down the steep hillside roads into Perth, unhindered by the heavy traffic on the A90.

Our little procession involved a number of additions including our new driver Lorna, and a number of Yes Bikers who would help support us along the remainder of our walk.

Arriving in Perth on the West Bridge street were well over fifty local supporters, waving flags and clapping for us as we walked along the footpaths alongside them.

Supporters came from Yes Perth City and Perthshire Pensioners for Independence. They included a number of familiar faces from the larger Yes movement, including local William Duguid, plus Lindsay Mccrea from Yes Edinburgh and Lothians who was documenting the event with his camera for The National.

We had our little unofficial procession through Perth's high street, concluding at the end of the pedestrianised zone. The walkers, exhausted from the day's hike, proceeded onto the stopping point at Blend Coffee Lounge in the town. The eighteen miles of hard slog had felt like double that.

As the walkers proceeded towards the cafe, Wren and Laura were joined by Catherine Roland and George Page with their huge smiles, offering us yet more 500miles badges and wristbands to distribute. Laura asked Catherine about her husband, as the walkers presumed she was married to George. Catherine laughed, clarifying that she was very good friends with George but wasn't married to him. We would later meet her husband Alan in Stirling on the old bridge.

Here we were happy to call it a day. The walkers all received a well needed cup of coffee and crashed on the comfortable couches. Lindsay Mccrea and Nicholas both took our group photograph. One of which would appear in the The National paper the next morning, indicating our process as far as Perth. We'd like to say thank you to the staff at Blend Coffee Lounge, especially Dagmara and Grant who also had their photo taken with Laura and her shield.

While relaxing at Blend coffee, we received thanks and donations from a number of members from Yes Perth, including Bonnie Ayeman, Pat Bedde and Jasmin McCormach. Thank you!

That evening we were ferried in two different vehicles to our home-from-home for the night. One of the local Yes supporters, had offered us the use of their mostly unfurnished house. No longer living there, they had recently put it up for sale. It was located in the middle of the countryside. The owner had been so kind as to put enough mattresses in each of the four bedrooms for all of us to sleep on. They had turned on the heating and hot water, left us chairs. And to top all their generosity, they had made us a wonderful home cooked dinner of pie and apple crumble to share between all the walkers and drivers, leaving it cooking in the oven for when we got there! They had also gone to the trouble of providing us with a refrigerator full of breakfast food for the next morning, plus tea, coffee and a huge container of milk.

It would be an understatement to say we were

dumbstruck at their huge generosity.

Dave and Laura started talking to the owner, trying to figure out why the house was for sale and both learned a very important lesson about the new clearances happening in the Scottish countryside today. This is where wealthy landowners make life hell for anyone they want off their vast estates. This happened to be a perfect example of this, where the home owner (on leasehold property) and their children had been threatened (receiving persistent physical and mental abuse) by the landowner and their gun toting associates. The family had been forced to move, in order to maintain their health and safety.

In all honesty, we could not publish any more details about our incredible saint and her wonderful kids, without the possibility of bringing more problems to this unfortunate situation. We do hope they found a buyer for their great house, in its beautifully serene location. We also hope they find closure and peace with their new direction in life. We all wanted to say a massive thank you again for everything you did for us.

In all that we had been through and seen along the walk, discovering first hand about the new clearances going on. It added yet another reason for our cause for supporting an independent Scotland, one that can finally make positive and much needed changes to land ownership.

We hope that the 500mile walkers can help bring attention to the distress that is affecting many of our tenant farmers. Each and every one of them are essential for putting the Scottish produce on all our tables.

We had ended the day realising that we had probably

solved the dilemma from the beginning of the day. It was likely that the landowners clout in these parts is why bags of Scottish potatoes usually display a union flag. It is highly unlikely that these tenant farmers have much say in this matter.

Food for thought and #KeepScotlandTheBrand.

# OFF THE BEATEN PATH
## FRIDAY SEPTEMBER 28TH

Everyone at the house got cleaned up, ate a hearty breakfast and enjoyed the opportunity to have a good cup of tea or coffee. We left the house as we found it, before getting into the vans to be transported through the rural back roads to Perth.

The walk today started with Dean, Jim, Karl, Laura and Wren getting dropped off outside the Blend Coffee shop. We proceeded to take the roads to the opposite side of Perth, along the footpath of the A93.

We talked to a few locals many of whom were interested in our event, handing out badges and plodded on to the outskirts of town. As we left Perth, we passed construction workers who recognised us and offered us some positive cheer. It felt good to be back in friendly territory and find folk who were following along in our adventure.

Laura stopped a guy walking his two dogs, asking if there was a toilet nearby - regretting the large amount of coffee consumed that morning. He recognised the 500 miles walkers and offered to take her to his home. Laura hailed down Lorna, saying she would need picking up in ten minutes while she went to Craig Braveheart's house nearby.

Stopping at a strangers house wasn't something Laura would normally have done, but as a 500 miles walker she felt safe with a member of the Yes family. Discussing this camaraderie, Laura forgot to pick up her diary - the book that contained all the names and receipts from the walk up to that point!

We got to the roundabout where the A93 meets the A9 and we were somewhat surprised to find there was still a visible footpath. Unfortunately it lasted the usual mile or so before abruptly stopping again for no reason. It was here that Nicholas caught up with the rest of us to finish the walk with us that day.

We walked on the grass verges, behind barriers and signs, until we really couldn't continue any further. Out of necessity, we choose instead to walk north west to Tibbermore before proceeding again in a more westerly direction.

There wasn't much by way of traffic along this road, but since Nicholas was walking with his flag, we were getting quite a bit of attention, and occasionally a bit of expected jeering.

The weather that day was partially cloudy with very little wind. This was perfect walking weather. Except that we were effectively in the middle of nowhere and were getting quite parched for a drink.

Before too long, we came across a garden centre, which also had a cafe/restaurant. It didn't take much convincing the five of us to stop for a quick cup of coffee and a relaxing chat.

Nicholas had discovered that our walk had been mentioned that morning in the Scottish Government.

A motion had been lodged in regards to Nicholas' Blockchain voting cause. He was over the moon, and we were all rather surprised that the "500miles walkers" had been mentioned in session. Dean paid the bill and we got back to our task at hand.

We kept on walking along the quiet country road. At one point a woman speedily driving her daughter along in their grey coloured Range Rover, almost ran some of us off the road. It seemed intentionally as they made no attempt to move over or slow down. Nicholas was caught off guard and outraged at nearly getting run over, while the rest of us had seen enough close calls at that point that we'd become somewhat numb to the problem.

We passed through "Dubheads" before stopping at an entryway to a field at a crossroads near Madderty. Here Lorna's van had parked up so we could grab a bite of food and a drink. The unexpected sunny weather had really made the hike take it out of us. We were now glad that we hadn't started the hike during the dry summer.

Earlier, Laura had been dropped off at Cafe Mimis in Auchterarder (to do more PR work) by Lorna, after stopping to pick her up from Craig's house. Lorna later returned to collect Laura so she could rejoin the rest of the walkers at this improvised rest stop.

We all continued along the same rural road, taking the road to the south that brought us to the B8062 in Kinkell Bridge. Dean took some photographs of walkers hiking over the bridge, before walking across the bridge and jumping in the van for a necessary patch and repair. His blisters had started playing up again. A short distance later he rejoined the group and the van drove ahead.

We continued our hike through the countryside into the seemingly conservative looking town of Auchterader and up the High Street. It was to be the end of the walk for the day.

Some walkers took the opportunity to visit the local toilets before everyone jumped in the van to go to our stop for the night.

The original plan today was to get to Aberuthven. Thanks to the usual lack of footpaths along the A9, it was not to be. This was why our target was moved to Auchterarder and covered a more substantial 21 miles in all. Expectedly, the daylight was starting to fade.

We were whisked off to a house in Dunblane. Our host, Emily Bryce, had offered to put on a wonderful dinner and a place for us all to put our heads down for the night.

We were greeted with lots of guests from Stirling Women For Independence and Yes Stirling. This included Fiona McIntosh, Allison Graham, Ann and Rick MacGregor, Sharon Gallagher, Catriona and Dave Whitton, Diane Lloyd-Williams, John MacLean and Greg Drysdale.

We all chatted in length about our travels. We realised afterwards that it must have been hard for everyone to understand that we really could not mentally grasp the distance we'd walked ourselves. Dave Whitton of Clydesider fame played his guitar and gave us a great sing-along. Dean in particular enjoyed singing along to a few songs by Christy Moore (from his album "Voyage"), an album he was quite familiar with.

After the additional guests left, the walkers started getting ready for the night. Some of us were to use our sleeping bags on a carpeted floor, but didn't mind at that point. Dean's bad back meant that the hard floor was the preferable option to a soft bed anyway.

Laura reconnected with her social media later that night. She received a message on Twitter saying she was missing something from the 500 miles walk. She hadn't even noticing her diary wasn't in her possession. The exchange of messages resulted in Craig sending the diary ahead to Lorna's home. Lorna would be visiting there in a few days time, when our drivers would swap over again. Laura was elated that the names and bookkeeping was not lost.

Dave Llewellyn, starting to watch a video on his phone while laying down on the floor with a pillow, fell asleep from sheer exhaustion before it had even finished playing. He kept laying in this position even after we'd shut off his phone and moved it out of harms way. Those of us sleeping on the living room floor then proceeded to try to get some sleep before the room was drowned out with snoring.

# ADVANCE ON STIRLING
## SATURDAY SEPTEMBER 29TH

The walk today started with Laura, Nicholas, Jim, Karl, Wren, Dean, James and the "Last Jacobite" in Auchterarder High Street. We all continued south west along the footpath and on to Orchil Road.

Fans of golf should be familiar with this area, as it leads to Gleneagles Hotel. It was here that we 'lost' Nicholas for a wee while as he went into the golf building to discuss the 500miles walk and Blockchain with management there. At this point, the walkers had no idea about Nicolas' business background. But his promotion to the larger hotels made sense when we did connect the dots later on.

The rest of the walkers plodded on, walking down the footpath on the road that cuts through the middle of Gleneagles Village and then the north western edge of the famous golf course. There was nobody else walking on the road so we kept on going at our usual pace. Nick caught up with us again after jogging a fair distance.

From Gleneagles to the T junction at the A822, we saw probably a dozen or so metallic grey Range Rovers, which we presume were involved with either the golf course or out on shooting outings (tourists?).

A cyclist who knew who we were proceeded to curse at us and sing "God Save the Queen" as loud as he could! Funnily enough, before we got to the end of the road at the A822, this guy did exactly the same thing in the opposite direction!

We should clarify, the point of the walk was for promoting Scottish Independence and Blockchain Democracy. Recent polls have discovered that vast majority of the Yes movement could not care less about the monarchy. But until we get our independence, it makes little sense to make any waves about abolishing the monarchy (because until then we simply can't) and give any soft Yes voters a reason to vote no.

To be honest, nobody involved with the walk cared a jot about the royal family. We thought he was making a complete idiot of himself and we had a good laugh at his expense. But it brought to light the simple fact that our nations inadequate understanding of Scottish history has resulted in this outcome. The British Empire has succeeded in controlling the narrative for generations, resulting in this level of blind faith

As any newly independent country should do, this should be one of many decisions to be put to the electorate. For some reason, the "Better Together" campaign and the pro-royalty folk at the Daily Mail & Daily Express seem to think we're all anti-royalty, which isn't entirely true. Scotland has a long history with monarchs that pre-dates the union, though few of us can see any benefit with the arrangement today.

The Yes campaign cannot assume a union with Europe will happen either. But most Scots believe that union would be beneficial for maintaining many of

Scotland's existing relationships that depend on it (three of them being whisky, food and oil). Again, this would require a decision made by the Scots after gaining independence from the rest of the UK (although we already know 62% are in favour of the EU after the Brexit referendum, so it should be a moot point).

It was so sad to see abandoned buildings in the area west of the golf course - evidence of the local clearances in full view. There is little doubt that the tourists milling around the area, being chauffeured around, have absolutely no idea of their significance.

Turning down the A822, we headed towards Braco. Just before getting onto Braco's main street, the road has a double bend over a bridge. Alongside the road bridge is another bridge known as the "Ardoch Old Bridge" that also crosses over the River Knaik.

Dave, Jim and the Last Jacobite were going to take the opportunity to cross the old bridge (at their own risk!) to get their photograph taken. For anyone interested in the area, the old bridge lead to Ardoch Roman Fort (and would have passed across the present day road). The perimeter of the fort can clearly be seen from satellite photographs of the area (try Google Maps).

In Braco, we took a trip to their wonderful village coffee shop. Here all the team of walkers and drivers took the time to enjoy a twenty minute break, before heading off again into the countryside.

Out of the shop, we double backed up Braco Front Street in order to take the first road heading west. This was another largely featureless winding country road, with houses randomly scattered along its length. But there were two houses that caught our eye - the first was a house who's inhabitants must have known we were coming as they were waiting outside and wished us well on our walk - obviously Yes supporters, as they were flying a Saltire outside. We later discovered it was the home of Ted Christopher of the Tartan Army Band.

Almost a mile later down the road was what we can only presume was their arch nemesis. A farmer who rented out their holiday home and saw pride in having a Union flag painted on their cast iron sign by the road. We wonder, with the current state of Brexit and the expected negative impact on farming, if they have reconsidering their choices yet.

We continued, along the country lane into Kinbuck where we met a young woman walking her dogs and was very happy to talk to us, enquiring about what we were doing.

A short while later, we were walking along the road when Nicholas, Karl and Wren (at the front of the walking pack) noticed a upturned sheep, unable to right itself. Karl and Wren dashed into the field to upright the sheep while Nick filmed it with his tablet for his YouTube channel. They continued into Dunblane with a proud smile.

Reaching the main road, the walkers proceeded into Dunblane on the footpath, taking a brief stop at the roundabout. The centre of the roundabout has a number of old metal signs and topped with a coat of arms. Here we took a number of photographs with the entire crew before proceeding through the town to take a brief break at the end of the main shopping street.

We got chatting to a number of locals, a few of which made donations and had photographs and selfies taken with us. It was here that Nicholas met up with a local Edinburgh University student, Scott Gillen, who enquired about Blockchain Democracy. He was the youngest person Nick had talked to on the subject. This could only mean that word must have been getting out.

We couldn't stay long before continuing onwards on the southerly road towards the main A9/M9 roundabout.

James Gill had joined us again to continue his walking adventure. He told us how he had often slept in some locations in the area. It became strangely apparent that James (originally from somewhere in SE England, now based in the Aberdeen area) roamed everywhere carrying only a book, a bus pass, some cash, a bite to eat, and his old fashioned pipe. He was quite a character, and at that point had probably already walked over 100 miles with us.

Many of us, bewildered as to where we had walked, were a little surprised when we finally reached the roundabout. This was the main roundabout where the M9 ends and continues as the A9 heading north. A common reference point for anyone driving north, as some of the walkers did on their way to Skye.

The realisation that many of us weren't that far away from "home" in the central belt, came as a huge relief. We'd really covered all that distance!

We continued along the A9's footpath to the south towards the Bridge of Allan, taking a brief break at a lay-by to grab a quick bite, a drink and fix up our feet.

We continued on through the town of Bridge of Allan, taking the opportunity to speak to a number of locals and tourists about our walk.

We also came across a chiropractor with an amusing sign in their window. It was a whiteboard with the most appropriate "Quote of the Week" message: "Walking is mankind's best medicine  - Hippocrates". We really wished we could have stopped in for a "tune-up", but sadly, duty called.

Onwards we went along the footpath that hadn't ended for a surprisingly long time, past the Wallace High School. We spotted the National Wallace Monument to our left, up on the brae. We took the right turn, following the A9.

Dean's wife had made the trip to meet up to spend the night together in Sterling. She surprised him at this point, having walked behind Dave (coming to meet us) so as not to be spotted. Dean was delighted to see her.

Everyone continued to the bridge where the support vehicles were waiting for us. Shortly after we arrived at Stirling bridge, we had a little ceremony, various people made a number of speeches including the Last Jacobite.  It was good to see Cath Rolland with her husband so we could put a face to the name. George Page joined us again too. As the sun was setting, many of us were waving our flags with pride across the bridge. We'd made it to Stirling. After walking hundreds of miles, we had something personal to celebrate. We were on the home run! Dave shared our little festivity on social media.

Almost everyone left in the two vehicles to return back to Dunblane again for another night at Emily's house. Emily had cooked a huge dinner for everyone and a second evening of song and conversation was enjoyed by all.

Dean and his wife left the group to go to a hotel in Stirling with his wife. Only to discover that the shower in his hotel room didn't work properly!

# TROUBLEMAKERS
## SUNDAY SEPTEMBER 30TH

The intention for today's walk was to start at 9am, everyone gathering at the old bridge in Stirling, to walk up to the castle for a photo-op, before proceeding out of Stirling and on our way to Cumbernauld. If only it had happened to that plan.

The morning started with everyone having a hearty breakfast before being transported to Stirling Bridge. All the walkers plus our additional local Yes supporters (totalling thirteen of us) casually walked into Stirling's old town.

Things quickly started to get quite surreal for what could only be described as "Scotland's young-at-heart rebels". Few of us were on the younger side of a half-century, and only just.

While the party of walkers were walking up the brae towards the castle, Lorna in the support van had driven up ahead to park at the castle car park to wait for them. Her van was white with Scotland and Indy-Biker stickers on it and a Saltire flag flying. Lorna got to the castle at about a quarter past eight in the morning on a Sunday.

Stirling Castle is operated by Historic Environment

Scotland (HES) and the entry gates to the castle were not expected to open to the public until nine thirty that day, so the car park was expectedly deserted and the only people there would have been employees.

The car park itself is out-with the locked entry to the castle. There were no signs of any way of preventing the general public from accessing the car park at any time of the day, or night. Walking up to the statue of Robert the Bruce that overlooks the castle walls and the city of Stirling was located in the very same car park.

When the support vehicle got to the car park, they parked up, before being told they couldn't stay there. Lorna proceeded to have a conversation with a Historic Scotland employee who quickly radioed their superior for backup.

At this point the walkers were almost at the castle car park and walked in unaware of anything amiss. Thirteen of us walked into the car park with the intention of having a group shot in front of the famous monument, with the castle wall in the background and then politely leave. Throughout these miles, we were walking for Scotland, and had every intention of leaving no trace.

When we arrived we were approached by a HES superior. Before the walkers even made it near the statue, the HES superior was demanding that the walkers leave immediately. We were told we had no right to be there and if we didn't leave then they would call the police. Undeterred by the baseless threat, various members of the walking party said politely, "please do" which resulted in a largely pointless and heated discussion.

For those who do not know about Scotland's laws regarding the right-to-roam, the car park for the castle is considered public property and any member of the public has the right to be there at any time.

The superior, for reasons unknown to us, was somehow expecting us to be the front of a parade of hundreds, if not thousands! Were that the case, they might have had a point, but thirteen? We were accused of being hooligans, which was a bit of a stretch!

Of all the properties that Historic Environment Scotland operates, many seem to have since noticed that Stirling is one that seldom, if ever, flies a saltire. Opting instead to always fly the union flag. It also comes as no surprise to find plenty of evidence online that the UK Government and Conservative party have held numerous private functions within Stirling Castle's walls. When this news hit social media, many didn't know what to think.

While the heated discussion with the supervisor continued, Nicholas released a quick film clip, which quickly racked up 40,000 views. Dean was writing a note for a reporter at The National before proceeding to get photographs of the monument. Frustrated but realising we were wasting time with this futile argument, the entire group got a photo, then left the car park without making any further fuss.

Not 200 yards down the brae, we were met by a now all too familiar police car, and not an ounce of worry from us, nor from them! We met up and had a chat.

We were politely told by PC Spencer, the local police officer that they had received a phone call by a very distressed woman mentioning about a group of people in the car park. He then immediately went on to say he had no idea why they had made that phone call, as "we had every right to be there". The organisation didn't have a legal leg to stand on.

We spent five minutes talking about the "incident" before thanking the officers and wishing them well. We continued down through Stirling's old town, taking photographs alongside the stones on The Back Walk before continuing onwards towards the Battle of Bannockburn site at the edge of Stirling.

In stark contrast to our encounter with Historic Environment Scotland, the National Trust for Scotland site didn't make any kind of fuss. Here we had no trouble at all taking lots of photographs and having our own private ceremony of sorts. Dean bought a mini Saltire flag from their shop in a small gesture of thanks, and stuck it in the pencil pocket on his hi-vis vest.

We continued on towards the roundabout that crosses the M9 before taking a brief break at the side of the road to talk to a number of people who had stopped to say thanks to us for everything, offering a donation for our costs. Thank you to each and everyone!

We crossed the M9 and walked on towards Denny. In Denny, we took the opportunity to stop in the only place in town that appeared open at midday Sunday - Greggs! After all these miles, I doubt that there's anyone that would have turned down a sausage roll (or few) and a steaming hot cup of coffee.

Reluctantly, we continued on into Bonnybridge before turning on to the Seabegs Road that ran along the canal. Again, the footpath disappeared, and we had to take a break at a car park along the road so that Dean and Wren could repair their feet.

At this point Dean's blisters were getting huge - and bigger than the blister plasters we had. Published on Twitter thanks to Nick's phone, they were getting to be

2 1/2 inches long and desperately needed draining. The badges we were wearing were the only thing we had on hand to pop them to make walking even bearable. Dean used one that he had on his vest, after sterilizing it with an alcohol wipe.

The biggest issue were that our blisters were located in the rear-outside corner of our feet - a difficult location to see without kneeling down and putting your feet flat on the ground. Persistence paid off and Dean was able to get mobile again. Everyone enjoyed a brief walking break by the canal, while the rain held off.

James Gill, who we presumed knew where he was going, decided to walk along the canal path instead of along the road only to meet up with us shortly.

The rest of us were directed to stick to the road into Allandale and onwards to Castlegcary on the road that runs alongside the M80.

We then followed the path onto the A8011 and hit a snag. The footpath stopped, leading all pedestrians onto "Old Cumbernauld". The support team were expecting us to go to Asda in "New" Cumbernauld. Somehow.

We all walked into Old Cumbernauld, meeting up again with James who decided to walk into the local pub for a quick drink, only to discover that this was a pub that wasn't particularly friendly to the Yes crowd (fortunate that he wasn't wear one of our hi-viz vests). The rest of us sat around near the shopping street wondering where to go next. Weren't we in already in Cumbernauld?

We didn't know the difference or how to get from one side of Cumbernald to the other, and our support drivers were getting angry because of it. In the end Lorna in the support vehicle drove back to the location where walkers were and not-so-politely told them to go back to the main road and walk down to Cumbernauld. So the walkers walked down the dual carriageway of the A8011, ignoring the pedestrian barriers trying to keep people off the road, in order to make it to the other side of Cumbernauld.

Again we have to mention the fact that we were not from the area, and nobody had done any real on-foot reconnaissance like this. When they built this road, there can't have been any plans for what pedestrians should do to get from one side of town to the other.

We've no idea why, but presumably for anyone to get from old to new Cumbernauld they must own a car or take a bus! This is the 21st century and we still have intentionally naive design choices like this to contend with. We saw no visible signs anywhere that would have helped us through the woods or around them.

Ignoring the visual cues for keeping pedestrians off the road, the team eventually made it to Cumbernauld's Asda car park where they made it up to 18 miles covered that day. To be honest, quite a few of us were quite annoyed about the lack of planning in this stage. Obviously there should have been some better way to get to the destination, and yet it was implied to be our fault for following the lousy environmental expectations. Tensions were rising, through no fault of anyone here.

Pedro Mendez with his girlfriend Eileen Hamilton were waiting in the car park to meet up with us. We were also joined by Joe Grant who had offered his services as an additional driver with his distinctive yellow box van.

Before leaving, some of the walkers ran into Asda for a stock-up on more ibuprofen and plasters! Many of the walkers were taking ibuprofen regularly - almost like a kid would eat Smarties. It wasn't as if we had much choice. Walking hundreds of miles without much of a chance for a break really hurts.

That night we were driven to Pat Lee's house in South Lanarkshire. Pat and his wife put us all up for the night and bought us all a fish-n-chips dinner (or whatever we preferred instead).

It was a cosy night. We were happy to be sleeping indoors as it was starting to become much cooler during the evenings.

Pat held a regular video conference call with a number of other Independence folk each week, on the *People's Indy Chat Show*. That night happened to be when the show was regularly broadcast.

Since we were all in Pat's living room, he had some of us speak for the group to his other guests and of course the rest of the audience listening online.

Pat is heavily involved with the *People's Doorstep Referendum* and this is how they discussed the latest Pro-Indy news and events. You can find them on Facebook at @DoorstepThe.

After the online call was over, it wasn't long before everyone got ready for bed and try to get some sleep most of us using our sleeping bags in the living room and dining room floor.

Everyone else in the room had to endure someone snoring and later complained they didn't get much kip. You can probably guess by now, who was held to blame.

# TO GLESGA
## MONDAY OCTOBER 1ST

A ll the walkers were ferried back to the same Asda
car park by Joe Grant and Pat Lee. It was another
8am start, continuing our walk from the same location
where we'd finished the day before. We met up with a
bunch of Yes Cumbernauld members. They wanted to
gather everyone together for a quick photo-op, before
the walkers had to leave. We were more than happy to
oblige.

We proceeded to walk through Cumbernauld town
centre and onwards through the housing development
with the assistance of a local resident. Cumbernauld
was obviously designed from the outset to separate
vehicle traffic from pedestrians, so we needed guidance
to make it from this side of town and out the other side.

"The Wildcats @catnev8" tweeted "Hats off to the
weary walkers. Passed them today in Cumber'd
conditions dry but Baltic! A truly stoic group". Yes it was
a chilly start, but we were ignoring it, knowing we'd be
fine when we got moving.

We traversed through Cumbernald's maze of
footpaths. Dave and Lorna were patiently paying close

attention to Dean's shared GPS location, trying to figure out the locations they had to drive to, in order to meet up with us again. The short-cuts were great for the walkers but frustrating to our support team.

Seafar Roundabout had been partially closed for major road resurfacing work. A few of the road workers were surprised to see us walking by, and appeared to know who we were. A few of them were more than happy to ring our freedom bell and get their photographs taken with Wren and Laura.

Our support team managed to catch up with us and tell us to avoid walking alongside the A8011 Glasgow Road. We had been hesitant to walk on it as it didn't appear to be safe to walk along. The approach road appeared to look not dissimilar to a motorway. We continued walking through the safer Greenfaulds neighbourhood instead.

After reaching the Condorrat Ring Road, we ran into three additional Yes supporters, Dainaila Glas plus Pedro and Eileen (who we first met at the Asda car park the previous evening). They posed for selfies with the walkers before walking with us into the town centre.

Dainaila Glas had been following the walkers on Facebook, and offered her local knowledge to lead the walkers towards Glasgow. This was a huge relief as numerous sections of roads into Glasgow were pedestrian free zones.

In Condorrat we were met by supporters Liz Purdon and Lorna Smith (who help organise Indy Girls) running out of their houses to meet up with us. A short while later, we all stopped in front of the three memorials. The whole walking party posed for photographs, prominently displaying Laura's saltire shield in front.

We should note the wording on one of these three

memorials, since it was important to our walk. It said:
"In memory of the Condorrat radicals who fought for democracy for all in 1820. John Baird - Radical Leader, John Barr - Weaver, Thomas McFarlane - Weaver, William Smith - Weaver, John Allan - Weaver. *Weave the truth.*"

The walking team chatted with our supporters for a short while before offering our thanks and goodbyes and continuing onwards through Condorrat. We took a turn at Kirk Place, up the hill and crossing the footbridge over the M80 that lead us all into the Westfield neighbourhood and walking along the main road.

The support vehicle finally met up with the walkers again when we all made it to Westfield Road. Heading west, we all curved around the corner where AG Barr makes Scotland's favourite fizzy drink and then took Mollins Road to head north west.

The footpath blessed our feet, but it wasn't long before it had disappeared again. Still we persevered walking into East Dunbartonshire, taking the B8048 towards Kirkintilloch. The conditions dictated that we were to walk in single file along the road.

Nicholas took a short video clip to advise everyone not to try to walk along roads like we had, because of the high likelihood of getting into an accident. The video clip actually caught a situation when Nicholas had a close call with a passing car. The road was horrible to walk on and we were thankful for having our high-visibility vests on. The irony on getting into Kirkintilloch was that underneath their town's sign was another official sign that said:

"A Walkers are Welcome Town"

How, we wondered, are walkers welcome? There's no footpath to get into Kirkintilloch from this side (and the same applied from most directions too)? We continued towards the downtown shopping street, trying to figure out how to get there using their pedestrian paths, devoid of any direction signs.

Once we got into the high street we noticed Rona Mackay MSP's office on Townhead - so we had to snap another selfie. Only afterwards did we discover that her office was in the process of moving further down the road. So we walked there instead. This time Rona Mackay MSP was there and came out to meet us, She was so happy to see us walking through Kirkintilloch and joined us for another group photo.

We proceeded along Cowgate a little further before we decided we needed to take a break for lunch. We stopped in Dnisi, one of the local cafés, for a bowl of soup and a sandwich to get our energy back. The hike so far wasn't too difficult, but the weather was overcast and threatening to rain.

We took an hour for lunch before continuing our walk through town and heading for Cadder, Bishopbriggs and Glasgow.

Dean had to bail out before even reaching Cadder as he had totally lost the ability to walk with his monster sized blisters flaring up again. He so called for support and jumped in the van. The rest of the team continued on following the footpath along the A803.

All was well until Springburn, where the A803 becomes a vehicles-only road, but with a little assistance from Dave and Dean in the vehicle and following signs along the road, they kept on walking along back paths through the housing development. Losing sight of the walkers, Dave tried to reconnect with them to help direct them as the A803 was not going to permit walkers for much further (nearer the motorway, it is signposted as no pedestrians). Since Dean was in the vehicle and had his phone on him, the GPS location Dave was tracking was the van and not the walkers! After figuring out what was going on, the support crew managed to meet up with the walkers again at Atlas Road, to tell them to follow the footpaths directed them to Glasgow's People's Palace Museum in order to meet up again with the driving crew.

The walkers continued unhindered, taking Castle Street which eventually leads towards Glasgow Cathedral.

The van was parked outside Glasgow's People's Palace Museum, where they waited for the walkers to approach and offered them all refreshments.

We all discovered after the fact that the original plan was to be walking into Glasgow a day later and end up in Kelvingrove Park. That would have resulted in a much more substantial crowd. But due to this slip of planning, the walkers had been delayed temporarily at the People's Palace location in order to make time to organise an impromptu setup at "Freedom Square" instead.

Mike Fenwick joined us and hiked with the walkers from the People's Palace to the "Freedom Square" whilst Fiona MacKinnon was simultaneously broadcasting live on Independence Live. Wren and Karl kept walking ahead, annoying Fiona who kept shouting to keep everyone together as a group in-camera!

Transported to "Freedom Square" in the van with Dave, Lyndsey and Lorna, Dean was there waiting for them to arrive. One foot was half out of his boot as he just couldn't stand on it, limping around while carrying his camera to catch the rest of the team's arrival. It was here that Dean decided that he had no choice but to leave and treat his blisters. He would take the next day out in order to be able to finish the rest of the 500 miles.

It wasn't long before the rest of the walkers walked into "Freedom Square" from the south west side, to be met with a cheering response from the hundred or so people waiting for them in the dreich weather. They had made it to the square by 5pm covering a total of 25 miles, all told. Two of the supporters who were there to meet the walkers included Wren's two daughters.

Stalls had been setup by two members of Athletic Angels with a sit-on massage chair ready for the walkers to use. A second stall selling 500miles badges, mugs and other promotional gear (which was meant to raise money to cover costs) was setup by George Page and Cath Rolland from Lomond Graphics & Promotions.

Various members of the walking team were interviewed live by Independence Live. Pilar Fernandez with Rosalía TV shot some video of Laura with her Catalan flag and was interviewed about her views on the situation in Catalonia (it was close to the anniversary of the referendum vote in Catalonia).

Scottish photographer Billy Knox who had been taking photographs to document all the Yes events since the first referendum, took photographs of the walkers at "Freedom Square".

Early on, Laura had stepped out a few times to do PR work and deal with her ankle injury, so knew she couldn't realistically cover every mile. But held to the concept that Dean had said at the outset - the 500 miles was a team effort and none of us were expected to walk every mile. But we had to finish.

Nicholas was required to miss three entire days of the walk early on when the walk went around the north-east of Scotland. His earlier absences were due to ongoing blockchain architecture work, building the underpinnings necessary to define (for media) that Scotland's blockchain academics in Edinburgh Napier University (who were on the verge of opening the world's first blockchain identity laboratory) had secured funding for democracy platform capability.

Jim told Nicholas, 'It's a shame that you missed those 3 days walking, because as at today, with 4 full days of remaining, you are *only* 160 miles short of the target'.

Nicholas then said to Jim, 'If I don't try it, I'll never know if I could do it'. He quickly grabbed his backpack and started running down the side of The Union Canal, heading east.

Over the next four days, Nicholas delivered a rapid fire twitter record of ongoing photographs and narrative, and maintained a steadily published stream of satellite navigation records which physically confirmed that he had successfully achieved the distance targets.

This enabled five of the original start line walkers, to have completed the full 500 miles distance. Nicholas would meet us again on the final full day of walking, at the mid point of The Forth Road Bridge.

Dean however was pretty devastated at this point, and there was no way he could continue with a 2 inch long blister on each foot, both an inch wide. His wife drove to Glasgow to pick him up. He took most of his gear home with him, knowing there would be no more camping adventures in the remaining days.

After spending an hour in Glasgow's "Freedom Square", the remaining walkers split up in to two groups for a place to stay.

Jim (who was in desperate need of a good night's sleep) and Laura went to stay with Jim's grandson, Fraser Stewart, at his place in Glasgow.

The rest of the remaining walkers spent the night at Karl's place beside Glesga Green.

For anyone wondering where "Freedom Square" is - it is the name most of the Yes movement use for the location instead of the current official name "George Square" (named after King George III). We would like to think that it won't be long before the square at the heart of Glasgow gets a new permanent identity.

# SHOWDOWN IN HARTHILL?
## TUESDAY OCTOBER 2ND

IS Í DING DI FÉIN A SCOILEANN AN DAIR.

A ll the walkers knew that today would be a problem. Warnings had been mentioned on social media before the 500 mile walkers had even travelled to Skye, mostly by locals who lived in the area. Harthill and surrounding communities had a history of being union flag waving areas. Getting through the region would likely require the help of a number of locals who knew the territory well. Nobody was looking forward to it.

We were one walker down (Dean was getting his feet sorted and spent most of the day soaking his feet in Epson salts) the rest were still eager to pound the pavement.

Pat Lee, Jim, Wren, Karl, Laura and Cliff were the walkers for the day. Ian McGlade from Yes Bellshill & Mossend (and also behind the Scottish Digital Covenant connected to the paper version that we had also been getting people to sign along the route of the 500 miles) joined the walkers and was our local expert guide for that days walk.

Dave and Lyndsey were in the support car, although Lyndsey would later walk part of the distance. Jim and

Laura showed up in a taxi with his grandson, who then had to do another round trip to return Laura's shield (Laura had forgotten it, at his place).

The walkers left Glasgow's Freedom Square at 9am sharp (at the demand of Jim who wasn't going to wait for anyone) with around twenty additional supporters who accompanied them and proceeded to head east out of the city centre.

The route out of Glasgow passed by the People's Palace and through Glasgow Green. Down Dalmarnock Road and onwards to the A724 towards Cambuslang.

Walking into Rutherglen, the walkers were met by a piper and members of the local community. Jim and Laura walked and talked with many of them along the way.

Margaret Ferrier joined the group to hike a section of the walk. Margaret was a huge independence activist and had run for the local SNP MP in 2015, missing by a small margin thanks to the Tories tactically voting for Labour to knock out her chances.

At 11am, the group stopped at Stacks Cafe in Blantyre. Pat Lee covered the bill for everyone's brunch. Stacks Cafe was short of a public toilet, which was a problem when the walkers had just had a bite to eat.

Across the road from Stacks Cafe, was a pub - the Stonefield Tavern. Jim and Laura removed their 500 miles hi-vis vests before leaving the cafe, walking across the road and walked into the pub. Jim quickly realised his idea to remove their identifying vests was the best decision he could had made - the walls of the pub were covered in union flags and Rangers signs. Trying not to look too distraught, he asked if they could use the toilets and was given a slow nod as if the barman recognised their faces. On leaving and given thanks, Jim received a nod as if to say "you'll no be back again".

The walkers proceeded down to the David Livingstone Memorial Centre, across the River Clyde on the metal bridge into Bothwell and headed across the M74 Raith Interchange before climbing the Belshill Road. At the top of the hill they were greeted by another party of Yes supporters.

Everyone gathered in the Cafe Hepburn in Belshill for lunch. This time Margaret Ferrier and Ian MacGlade paid for the meals, while the owners offered the walkers their drinks for free. Margaret Ferrier had to leave at this point having walked from Rutherglen.

A lady bust into the cafe with two full carrier bags of biscuits and said "I saw you go past and thought I had missed you. I swept up the biscuits from my cupboards and raced up to find you"! Jim loved the gesture, bursting out laughing at the fact that Margaret's husband would be without any biscuits tonight. Laura and Jim chatted with her giving her thanks for her warm Glaswegian "shirt off your back" offer.

Across the street, a couple saw and crossed to meet with the walkers and walked with them to the end of Mossend, Bellshill. Leaving Bellshill the walkers entered Holytown and from there headed towards Newhouse on the Edinburgh Road along the A8 (which runs parallel to the M8).

Along the way the walkers were met by Martin Aiken and Martin McMahon - the organiser of the freedom convoys. The walking group reached Newhouse and headed towards Salsburgh.

It was decided that Salsburgh was going to be the

final destination for the walk that day, in order to prevent an unnecessary and unsettling confrontation in Harthill (located a few miles further down the same road). The new plan was to complete the hike by gathering on a footbridge that passed over the M8, waving Saltire and Yes flags to the passing cars - as the "Yes M8 Scotland" team had done on numerous occasions before.

Wren and Karl had walked ahead of the group again with Pat, following the main road and stopped after reaching the M8 bridge on the east side of Salsburgh. They would later discover that they had gone a little too far ahead and had stopped at the wrong bridge!

Laura, Jim and Iain McGlade (@YesM8Scotland), plus two councillors and another nine "Bridges for Indy" supporters had met up on the main street of Salsburgh before walking as a group, along a track that would lead to the Salsburgh footbridge.

It was Jim and Laura's first experience with Bridges for Indy, waving flags that Iain had brought for them to use, trying to get positive responses from vehicles on the M8 below.

Apparently the flag waving event had been published online a week earlier, for supporters to meet us after 4pm and bring their own flags. The walkers, being largely out of touch with social media, had absolutely no idea. But it was a much more pleasant end to the day than any of them were expecting.

Pat Lee, who had pre-arranged to leave his car in the area before leaving for Glasgow, picked up the group of walkers (from both bridges) and drove everyone back to his place nearby.

Nicholas' flag, from a custom image created by
"Brave" (@defiaye) depicting all the followers of
@YesDayScotland.

# TO LINLITHGOW
## WEDNESDAY OCTOBER 3RD

The plan today was to start the walk at Polkemmet Park (a little to the east of Harthill) before walking towards Whitburn. This is the park alongside the M8 where many folk wonder about the 51ft-high swan neck steel horn (that looks like a it would be at home on a Teletubbies film set) pointing across the M8.

Dean was dropped off by his wife so he could rejoin the group now that he had fixed up his feet. Cliff Serbie was leading the walkers along this section of the route. We collected our water and snacks for the day from the support van before walking down the quiet road skimming the top of Whitburn, before heading north on Station Road to Armadale.

The weather this morning was a typical autumn damp and dreary day. At the start we were blessed with pavements to walk on, but this soon disappeared because apparently nobody walks between Whitburn and Armadale. We'd like to beg to differ.

The walkers hiked into Armadale, past the car dealership to a roundabout that wasn't on any of our maps. This meant an educated guess about which way to go.

None of the walkers had any idea what to expect to find in Armadale. The only thing many of us remember, was feeling sorry for the run down state of so many buildings in that part of the town. We would have gone into town and walked down the High Street, but we were safer staying away from the A89 due to the pedestrian-unfriendly traffic levels.

The 500miler's continued into Bathgate before inadvertently splitting up into a couple of teams. Understandably, the ladies needed a bathroom break, walking off towards the local Aldi store. The rest waited for them at the roundabout at the bottom of Bridge Street before slowly progressing up the hill to see if Wren and Laura had walked through the back of Aldi towards town. Dean and Jim walked ahead a little to the pedestrianized area for a sit down and wait for them there.

It started raining, then got heavier. Laura met up with Jim and Dean and stepped into Costa to get out of the rain and grab a quick cup of coffee and a sandwich. Outside it would appear that Karl and Wren had simply continued walking along the A89 as if walking on auto-pilot. Cliff had not noticed them leaving again.

This was a problem because we were supposed to head north, not continue east. Now everyone left in Bathgate town centre was scrambling to figure out if anyone had Wren or Karl's phone number while trying to avoid getting wet in the rain shower. Eventually we did manage to get through to Karl. Lorna went to pick them up in her van. Finally regrouped at the edge of town, we continued walking to Torphichen.

Little did we know at the time, but this was a

surprisingly easy B-road to walk along, and while it had quite a few winds and bends, it had a footpath which made for a very pleasant hike. We'd been spotted on the walk outside Bathgate by The National's cartoonist Greg Moodie who drove past and waved at us - planning to meet up with us later.

We stopped briefly in Torphichen, where we had a chance to chat with some locals who were there waiting for us in the bus stop to Linlithgow. They all seemed quite impressed at our accomplishments with our 500 miles walk (which for a little village that gives an impression of being a Tory stronghold, was quite unexpected). Greg Moodie tweeted that we'd "been and gone. Fast walkers. Commendably non-slack". @ BagPurse tweeted "Torphichen welcomes the 500 miles walkers - thanks to Liz Pender for the pics @ YesWestLothian".

We continued on, joining the A706 and walking on towards Belsyde. Waiting at the entryway to the Belsyde Country House were a few supporters from Linlithgow who had been scouting where we were on our walk, so they could inform others about our expected arrival time to reach Linlithgow.

As we got to the first roundabout at the edge of Linlithgow, Lucy Noble approached and greeted us with a couple of other supporters from Yes West Lothian and walked alongside us, into town.

Walking into Linlithgow along Mains Road leads to the Black Bitch Inn. Here everyone seemed to run out of steam. We stopped and sat at the statues across the street where we met up again with Pilar Fernandez. Pilar wanted to interview some of us. Afterwards some of us stopped in the pub and Dean bought Wren, Laura and Jim a small drink.

At this point it was around 3:30pm, and Cliff's plan had been to get to Linlithgow and visit Linlithgow Palace. But in traditional fashion, nobody who went in the pub had a clue about this plan. Laura got talking the talk to the locals, and received another donation.

As it was now October, Historic Environment Scotland had reverted to its Winter hours, which meant Linlithgow Palace closed at 4pm. Cliff regrouped the walkers to proceed down the street. It was just after 3:45pm when we arrived and their security had denied access to us.

Dave proceeded to record a live video for social media, indicating we'd been denied access. Then Wren had an unexpected outburst at the sight of the text on one of the nameplates on the wall.

The entryway to Linlithgow Palace has number of nameplates, each denoting a King or Queen since Mary Queen of Scots. Why any of these plaques are on a Scottish historical site makes you wonder. Is it appropriate for England to remind Scotland about the English monarchy? Dave stopped recording, deleting his video to protect Wren's privacy.

At the statue at the foot of the brae, Linlithgow journalist Lorna Johnston read out a poem that she had written for the walkers (see opposite page).

We all gathered to grab a coffee at the Cafe Bar 1807 to recover from the day's events before we all got rides to places to stay for the night. Neil Cameron had joined us, as had Pilar Fernandez and her husband.

After a relaxing cup of coffee and a good chat with local supporters, everyone was whisked off to various different members of the local Yes community for a meal and a place to sleep.

They walk fur independence
They'd crawl upon their knees
That's why this walks important
Fur awe, like you an' me.
It started from there, up in Skye
An' ends in Edinburgh
Where staunch independence supporters gether
Wi' yin anither.
Drawing in the crowds, alang the way
They share a common goal,
That spurs the heart
An' soul.
Independence
Is whit they crave
From the cradle
Tae the grave.
So welcome tae ye's everyone
Whaw walk this road together
Ah ken you're there tae gie yer awe
So gie it hell fur leather.
You've walked awe in
500 miles
So mony folk
Charmed an' beguiled.
A truly great
Amazin' brand
Indepencence fur ⚑ Scotland
Leavin' footsteps in the sand.
So celebrate
This greatest feat
Independence forever
It's whit ye cannie beat.

© Lorna Johnston - October 3rd 2018.

Dean and Laura stayed with SNP Councillor Pauline Clark at her home in Briech. The drive there covered a lot of miles we'd just walked along that day. Eventually we past Briech's train station, which Pauline was so proud of, being instrumental in retaining it from closure.

Jim got to stay with Sheena Aston and her husband. They had a bottle of brandy that was first opened when they married and only opened on special occasions. Jim was privileged to receive a dram before the bottle was returned again in the cabinet. Jim said they were "a lovely lovely couple", "both in their seventies and ardent activists".

All the walkers were so grateful for the incredible hospitality offered by all to everyone that night. Thank you all.

# ONWARD TO QUEENSFERRY
## THURSDAY OCTOBER 4TH

Today was a huge mental relief - the end of the road was within grasp. Everyone now felt physically fit enough to get there. But first we had a task to complete.

Everyone returned to Linlithgow for about 9:30am and at this point a number of walkers tried again to walk to Linlithgow Palace. This time, the gates were open, but there was a Historic Environment Scotland employee there acting as guard.

This was unusual. Dean had actually visited Linlithgow Palace just a few weeks prior to starting the walk, and there were no more than three employees working there then - no security presence - all HES employees were working inside the actual palace building.

Cliff, Dean, Laura, Jim and Lorna Johnston (with her iPod recording the event) proceeded to try to get through the gates. Dean had his camera and Cliff, Laura, Dean and Jim were wearing their hi-vis vests. Dean however still had a Yes badge on his vest amongst others. The security guard tried to play hard-ball by trying to deny us access, complaining that the badges were political. The walkers were responding that the yes movement wasn't a political movement, which had just been recently proven in court. This proceeded for a few minutes before Dean started to take off badges to get past this impasse and Cliff used the distraction to walk past the guard, quickly followed by Jim, Lorna, Laura and then Dean. We simply had the intention of having our photograph taken in front of the monument, and that was all we were there for.

At this point Dean and his wife were still members of Historic Scotland. But their family membership was terminated later that day when Dean's wife failed to get an acceptable response from HES that included an apology for their provocative nature in handling the last visit. That apology was never received, only a generic 'doing our job' form letter.

While walking around the courtyard, Jim spotted a photographer shooting us from the roof of Linlithgow Palace and it would appear that we were being closely monitored. Why, we've no idea, as they were all made well aware of what our peaceful intentions were, the size of our party and knew we were also fully aware of our legal rights. We exercised our rights - having our photographs taken in front of the statue and building (never actually setting foot in the palace itself). Then we left, politely, offering a thank you for their time.

A little additional background is needed here for anyone who has not had the opportunity to visit Linlithgow Palace. The only building totally inaccessible *after hours* is the palace building itself. The grounds are shared with Saint Michael's Parish Church. Pedestrians can always enter the grounds and see the statue, via car parks located at either side of the grounds, as well as via the church. The main gate is meant only to stop vehicles entering the car park in front of the palace. This meant that the action of patrolling this gate was planned.

How sad that HES's actions have alienated native Scots, that they profess to serve. Is it HES's job to secure a historical narrative that puts Scotland second? It certainly appears to be the case where the British establishment takes precedence. Why HES thinks that a group that promotes Scotland would choose to inflict damage to property that belongs to Scotland, is anyone's guess.

The rest of the walkers who didn't want to go back to Linlithgow Palace were waiting at the foot of the palace ramp. The proceeding incidents had upset them enough that they had no intention of ever returning to the site.

We proceeded on foot out of Linlithgow, accompanied by a few local Yes supporters heading east and up the hill, past the train station, on the B9080.

This country road felt like a peaceful retreat with its continuous footpath and the incredible views of the new Queensferry Crossing and Forth Bridges on the horizon. We were grateful that the weather had been much dryer that day, and the outlook looked promising.

The country road lead to Winchburgh, which has a number of new housing developments. On the veranda of one of the new houses was a resident proudly waving a Saltire and Lions Rampant for us. If you're reading this, you've no idea how proud it made us feel to see this. Cliff was so impressed he dropped a 500 miles badge through his letterbox in appreciation.

While we where here we ran into another group of Yes supporters including Lucy Noble and Jacqueline Watson (flying their huge Saltire flag that said "For Scotland", "St Andrew" "And Freedom") on the opposite side of the road watching our arrival. So we stopped for a quick drink at the local Tally Ho Hotel before continuing east towards the town of Kirkliston.

It was an uneventful walk into Kirkliston before taking a sharp turn and heading north towards Queensferry. We walked over the bridge that traverses the M9, near the point where you can see the old road to the Forth Road Bridge still exists today. Some of the walkers accompanying us that day were starting to get weary, unfamiliar with the march-like pace that was now the norm for the walkers. Cliff, Wren and Karl wandered off into the distance while Jim, Laura and Dean kept back to keep close to our Indy supporting friends and taking a wee rest at the bridge.

We all reached Queensferry's main street by 3pm. We took a break and had a number of photographs taken with the bridges in the background and local Yes supporters. Thank you to Lindsay Mccrea for stopping to see us, and for helping to document it.

It was here that we became aware of a huge change of plan. Since we had somehow gained a day (we still didn't know how or what day things went awry, but presume it was around Dundee), the original plan was that we would arrive in Queensferry before leaving for Edinburgh the next morning to meet-up with the start of the Edinburgh All-Under-One-Banner march. But the march was on Saturday and tomorrow was Friday.

The "500 miles" was meant as a general target. During planning, Dave had taken into account that some days would be shorter, while other days would be longer, and over the course of three weeks, he expected the planned walk would cover closer to 570 miles. The route we had taken was roughly based on a map provided by the Yes Bikers. They had measured the distances and driven the route. We'd had a few days cut shorter than we'd expected plus a few detours (due to the dangers of being on foot). So even though we didn't have an accurate figure of miles walked, we thought it might be possible that individually, we might be a few miles short.

We were told that the Yes supporters in Fife were annoyed that we'd missed them out of our scheduled plans. And also that the Yes Hub in Kirkcaldy had just opened that week. We had an extra unplanned day so we would give supporters in Fife their wish and walk the entire distance to Kirkcaldy. We figured if we were short of any miles, then that would easily make up the difference.

What wasn't planned for was where to sleep for the night. Dean, offered to take Jim and Laura to his home in West Linton. His house had space for more, but only one car and West Linton wasn't exactly nearby. Dean's wife drove to pick up Jim, Laura and Dean and drove them to West Linton.

That night Yes Linton happened to be having their monthly committee meeting. Dean's wife was expected to turn up to the meeting to brief the Yes group on the walkers progress. Entering the room, she excused herself for arriving a little late. Then behind her, the three walkers surprised everyone with their unexpected visit, rendering the meeting agenda cancelled as we talked about our endeavours.

One of the committee members also works for The National. So the 500 mile walkers made front page news again, sharing the story about the hassle from

Historic Environment Scotland staff at Linlithgow Palace. This was published in the paper on Saturday - march day - because we'd missed the deadline for a Friday printing. Alongside the article was a photograph of the three 500 mile walkers in front of almost all the Yes Linton members at the meeting. Thank you Deb for the group photograph.

The rest of the walking team stayed in Edinburgh. Lyndsey stayed with Lorna at her place, while Dave drove home to his. It had been a very productive day, even though we'd only covered a "brief" 11 miles of walking.

# CATCHING UP
## OCTOBER 2ND - 4TH

Nicholas left the rest of the gang after meeting them in Glasgow's "Freedom Square" and realising that his efforts to work on Blockchain Democracy during the walk had resulted in him missing out around 160 miles, at this point. Nicholas was unwilling to finish without completing the goal of 500miles that he'd started with.

Nicholas was no stranger to long distance running, having competed in the Ironman challenge before, but the next few days would require him to push himself to do TWO marathons per day in order to catch up with the other walkers.

Along the way, Nicholas encountered a number of supporters across Fife. Here's a few of them:

Steve Murdoch told us he met up with Nicholas at Tentsmuir Forest.

On October 3rd, Nicholas tweeted, "Blood on the front inside of the kilt? #GoFigure Feet now blistering... Without support driver Duncan Hogg today, this would already be #GameOver "

During his 160miles challenge, Nicholas tweeted using his @YesDayScotland account with the hashtag: #160miles

Steven Brown of @thecourieruk ran into Nicholas and asked "Can we have a #160miles ultra interview?" Nicholas responded, "By all means. Providing you can write at 6.5 kilometres per hour!". An article was published a few days later in The Courier on October 5th.

# HELLO KIRKCALDY
## FRIDAY OCTOBER 5TH

The gang was back together, meeting up at the car park that sits at the south side of the Forth Road Bridge. We were all there for the crack of dawn for the walk in.

James had rejoined us again. Presumably Dave told him our plans again which made the rest of us start to wonder - did James know more about the plan than the rest of the walkers?

The weather started off chilly but glorious, with barely a cloud in the sky. If we didn't have a farmers tan yet, then the conditions today would likely fix that.

Everyone started walking down the stairs from the viewing deck and followed the footpath across the old road bridge. Someone on the road below noticed that Cliff was flying a saltire and shouted at him asking why. Cliff had to tell them that we were walking for Scotland, to which he was offered appreciation. Before we had got a quarter way onto the bridge, Nicholas had rejoined us, running to catch up with us - now with painful blisters from his challenging 160 miles catchup.

We all walked on over the bridge, following the

footpath through Inverkeithing before proceeding on the
A921 and through Hillend. As usual some of the major
roads were lacking a public footpath, but we'd given up
caring and plodded on.

While walking through Aberdour, we came across
a woman who was loading things into her car and
wanted to chat to us. So we did until she discovered
that we were walking for Scotland and promoting the
Yes movement. In a moment of obvious British tabloid
headline recital we heard "You should give it up already.
It's over." We all carried on, figuring this "conversation"
had hit a terminal end.

Continuing into Aberdour, Jim tried to see if he could
find a newsagents that had a copy of The National
- eventually finding the last copy - or was it the only
copy? Jim seemed to think not, and the shopkeeper
seemed happy about his purchase. Perhaps Aberdour
was a Tory stronghold and they were starting to see
past that? We can only hope after Brexit kicks in.

We met up with the support van again. Lorna told us
the route instructions to follow the A921 in Burntisland
towards the shore where it takes a zigzag backwards
on itself to continue towards Kinghorn.

Nicholas and Laura must have missed the chance to
talk to Lorna because they both took the shorter scenic
over the hills version along the B923 Birch Avenue
route instead. Laura wasn't impressed with the hills.
Nicholas and Laura later reported having a near death
experience on this section of road, clinging on a verge
inches wide, when a very quickly approaching lorry
did not slow down. In complete contravention of The
Highway Code.

A passer-by shouted something that caught Jim off guard, only for Dean to realize it was his friend, Gavin, from West Linton and he knew this area well. Stopping for a brief chat we had to continue on before meeting Gavin again later that day.

We walked through Kinghorn, briefly made famous for the local blacksmith's patriotic sculpture "The Flag Bearer", a silver figure that clutches a St. Andrew's Cross flag. It sat atop the Archway Metals building, made by Andy Davies. The statue looked wonderful, and we're sad to discover that Fife council was trying to have the statue removed. Once again another example of how Scotland's unionist councils keep proud Scots down, all because of a saltire. We're sorry to hear that Fife council won that fight, but can only presume those days are numbered and the Flag Bearer will one day return.

Reconnecting the group after a walk through Kinghorn, we started diverging into two groups again - Cliff, Wren and Karl went ahead at their faster pace, while Dean, Jim and Laura kept at a slower pace.

Dean remembered Jim mentioning "What's the hurry?". We had to meet up in Kirkcaldy after 4pm, which we'd easily be able to make, simply by walking at a more leisurely pace.

Everyone met up again at the Kirkcaldy Lorry Park, where the two support vehicles were parked - waiting for the right time to walk to Scotland's latest "Yes Hub". The local cafe served what could only be described as lorry park food - and after 3 weeks on the road, it tasted braw!

Dean met up again with Gavin and had a good chat. Gavin wanted to go to the march in Edinburgh, but had obligations in the morning setting up the farmers market in West Linton that he and Dean would usually setup the first Saturday each month. Based on the numbers we'd heard about, Dean shared that the start would likely take hours, so Gavin should still be able to make it and apologised for being unable to help volunteer with the monthly market chores.

We all gathered and wandered along Kirkcaldy's front, before walking into town and meeting up with the Kirkcaldy Yes group at their new hub "Yes 2 Scottish Independence" on Hunter Street.

There we had an opportunity to have a group photograph outside the Kirkcaldy YES hub. It would appear that our arrival coincided with a bunch of unionist supporters, who unsuccessfully tried to get some attention. Fortunately they left on their own accord. Some of us didn't even notice they were there. A strange benefit to being in "the zone", we had succeeded in making the staunch unionists frustrated at accomplishing our seemingly impossible goal.

We were greeted by a dozen local Yes supporters including Peter Grant MP, and invited inside for fresh cups of tea, coffee and home made cake. It was a wonderful greeting and their new Yes hub made some of us envious, wishing our communities could do the same.

After spending an hour at Kirkaldy's new hub, we were whisked off to our accommodation for the night. The walkers had all been offered dinner and complimentary accommodation at the Balbirnie House, at Markinch village, located in the geographic heart of Fife.

In context, Balbirnie House was host venue for Scotland's inaugural #BlockchainDemocracy summit, in March 2018.

This was a wonderful way to spend the last night of our 500 miles walk, with the one major problem - we had to be ready and up at 4am to be at Queensferry's Main Street for our six o'clock start.

# LAST LEG INTO AULD REEKIE
## SATURDAY OCTOBER 6TH

I SCATH A CHÉILE A MHAIREANN NA DAOINE.

Nobody wants to wake up at 4am, especially after spending the night in probably the most upscale hotel many of us have ever set foot in. We'd like to say thank you to Nicholas for the generous hospitality.

Lorna and Cliff's girlfriend were our drivers for the last trip to our starting point. We were all very tired and unprepared for such an early start. Still we all knew this was it - the last leg and we just had to complete the task at hand. Unsurprisingly, we were all very cranky.

We arrived on Queensferry's main street and tried to stay quiet. It was strange to see it so deserted and quiet. We were joined by Pilar Fernandez and Neil Cameron, both there to walk with us on our last leg into Edinburgh.

The sky was still pitch black and only a few of us had thought to bring a torch to use. The hike out of Queensferry is a typical unlit 'B' road. But this one was blessed with a footpath and that eventually connects with the A90 which also happens to have a footpath! The City of Edinburgh was considerate to pedestrians!

We marched towards the edge of the city. By the time we got to the A90, the sun had started to come up. We proceeded on towards Cramond Brig where we met up with a dozen additional walkers who were joining us for our stroll into the city. We waited for a short while and set up our flags before marching onwards.

Continuing along the A90, taking the split at Hillhouse Road and headed SE towards Craigleith Retail Park where we were scheduled to gather and wait for more to join our walking party.

Before getting to the Craigleith Retail Park, we came across three pensioners, one of which thought it strangely acceptable to shout "Seig Heil" and give the accompanying salute.

We thought it was beyond belief and a sad sight to see. It was obvious he didn't understand what fascism actually meant. We shouldn't need to remind anyone that the desire for Scottish Independence has nothing to do with party politics and political stance. But the obstacle to getting Scottish independence is now most certainly being blocked by actual fascists.

We had witnessed someone who had been conditioned to believe this narrative, as dictated by the relentless propaganda and PR from the British Government's increasingly myopic and relentless media empire. It is exactly how Brexit won the vote.

We arrived at Sainsbury's around 8am. The majority of the group took the opportunity to grab a coffee. For many of us, this was the best cup of coffee we'd had in weeks - certainly the first we had the luxury of time to enjoy it. More people joined the walking party, including the Independence Live crew and Pedro Mendez dressed up like a pirate, channelling Jack Sparrow of *Pirates of the Caribbean* fame. After the walkers were all interviewed live on Independence Live, we continued our saunter towards Edinburgh.

Along the 500 miles walk, Pilar had been talking to the various members of the 500 miles team, gleaning information from us for inspiration on her media channels. This time, Dean finally had the opportunity to talk with Pilar Fernandez at length and share thoughts and stories as our growing walking group all walked towards Dean Village.

We continued through a short cut that lead to Charlotte Square and on towards Bute House. It being Saturday (and the First Minister doesn't actually live in Bute House) we didn't realistically expect to see or hear from anyone official. But this didn't stop us from stopping and having a number of speeches to celebrate the 500 mile walkers making it to this important destination.

Bute House provided the opportunity for a commemorative photograph of the 7 walkers who had started together on The Isle of Skye. Wren's dog "Badger" also made it into the photo!

It really is an interesting comparison to see the freedom of access to the steps of Bute House, when compared to the equivalent in London that has been strictly off limits to the pubic since the mid 1980's. Perhaps this is meant to be a sign of Scotland's intent to fully embrace freedom?

Laura Marshall provided a quick LiveIndyScot interview on the steps of Bute House, talking about a forthcoming blockchain powered poll on Scotland independence. Nicholas was procedurally unable to do this on the day, due to working on an 'exclusive' for Truly Scottish TV.

At around 11:30, once we'd completed our tasks

outside Bute House, we walked south towards Princes Street, crossing it and walking up Castle Terrace to wait at Johnston Terrace.

Dean had met-up with his wife, who had brought his Cameron Modern kilt, and changed from wearing trousers (only the second time in 3 weeks) into a much more appropriate and traditional 8 yard kilt for the remainder of the day.

We assembled at the foot of Johnson Terrace. It was such a stunningly beautiful Scotland early Autumn day, not a cloud in the sky, in contrast absolutely to some of the weather conditions we'd experienced over the three previous weeks.

Everywhere we looked, all who had been involved with the 500miles project, were either talking to cameras, or recording smart phone memories, or chatting with people who we had met at some point on the walk. Making our way up through the quickly assembling crowd on Johnston Terrace, was a completely surreal experience. It was obvious that there were already thousands of Yes supporters here. We could barely make it to the top of the brae as the crowd was so dense.

Arriving into the massive crowd outside The Hub at the roundabout at the top of The Royal Mile, was even more surreal. The mass of people had already become so densely packed you could feel an absolute sense of positive energy and determination. It was such a joyful and peaceful celebration of what Scotland's future could become.

There were young and old. So many people had brought their children. Memories of a lifetime for everyone there. Some were frail and yet so strong in their dogged determination to be part of this. A low and resonating hum, a force of massed and joyful energy. The sheer amount of noise was becoming deafening. Dust rising into still air, spiralling in shards of golden sunlight. A breathtaking, astonishing, totally stunning emblazoned sea of flags in shades of blue, a celebration of Scotland, the humour, the culture, the people. The welcoming and embracing Scotland we know we already are, one of tolerance, and holistic inclusion.

Many of the 500 miles project team had been on many of the previous independence marches during 2018's summer of gathering momentum. The energy and scale of Edinburgh's Royal Mile, was something none of us had ever seen before. Dave, like many of us, admitted he was having a hard time fighting back tears of joy and being overwhelmed.

Along the walk, Dave had made mention of us forming a human saltire, where we'd wear white and form a cross with blue in the middle and walk down the Royal Mile like this. At any other march, that could have been a feasible task. With thousands and thousands of people all ready for the Edinburgh march to start with barely an inch left to stand, forming anything of the sort wasn't going to happen.

At 12:50pm - ten minutes early - the front of the march started moving forward and the pipers and drummers started playing their music. The wheelchairs were pushed forwards and we started to move, right behind them.

Before we'd even reached the first cross-street at George IV Bridge/Bank Street, we could see that people had joined in the march in front of us - so many in fact that you could no longer tell where the front was. The cross traffic also introduced gaps, and at one point Dean was leading a section of marchers, holding his Saltire on a five meter flagpole with a grin on his face from ear to ear.

Dean ran into Leslie Riddoch and she asked him to have a selfie with her which she quickly shared on Twitter. Everyone in the group met with MSP Christine Grahame at some point down the mile. Dean also met with his local SNP councillor Heather Anderson. It would appear that every almost Holyrood politician and councillor we'd met along the way, was here today.

The 500miles walk had generated very significant mainstream media attention, and none of us could even hazard a guess at the accumulated scale of the social media footprint.

The walkers were still wearing high-vis vests emblazoned on the back with Cliff Serbie's instantly recognisable "500 miles walker" wording, and logo. Throughout the march down the Royal Mile, fellow marchers behind and to the side were asking us, one after the other, about the walk itself, passing on exuberant and heartfelt congratulations, which was profoundly humbling. We felt so proud.

At Holyrood, we'd hoped to have some sort of meeting with someone from the Scottish Government, but this was not to be.

Footage later released on the YesDayScotland media portal had definitive moments recorded outside Scotland's Parliament. The camera rounded the corner between a deeply worried and overwhelmed Conservative List MSP, Annie Wells (hoisting her solitary union flag) and moved on to capture 500miles organiser Dave Llewellyn being spontaneously embraced by those who had been met during the walk. What a celebration!

And what a well-deserved welcome for Dave, whose adaptive planning overview, had somehow gotten everyone through to the end. Truly remarkable scenes. The Edinburgh march wound its way past Scotland's Parliament, and into Holyrood Park. What a momentous gathering, and what a statement of intent for the future.

Scotland's YES bikers cranked their engines and starting filtering through the road in procession through Holyrood Park. That procession of motorcycles alone, took a full ten minutes to make its way along Queen's Drive.

In the previous week, the Independence march organisers had been working with Police Scotland and Historic Environment Scotland (who were legally tasked with maintaining Holyrood Park) for permission to use the park as a destination for the march. That permission was implied based on the social media posts left by the organisers. When we got to Holyrood Park, we walked to the stage that had been setup on the grounds to the back of Holyrood Palace. When we got there, we rested on the bank to the left side of the stage. We met up with a number of Independence 'celebrities' including a number of politicians for the SNP.

The park kept filling up, and the speeches kept on going. Gavin who we'd met the previous day, later divulged that he made it to the beginning of the march at 2:30pm. The crowds were still coming down the Royal Mile and hadn't stopped!

It was an incredible sight to witness over two hours after we'd started. Based on timing and scale of the

2018 All Under One Banner march, stated by official police numbers, the YesDayScotland media portal defined Edinburgh's numbers in the region of 130,000 that day. What we do know is that Edinburgh has never had a march that lasted so long before.

During and after the walk, the 500 miles walkers and crew met so many of the people who we met during the previous weeks. They travelled to Edinburgh from all across Scotland. By then, it was fully beginning to be understood in a totally unexpected way, that all involved had been on the receiving end of hospitality, sustenance's and shelter. It made us more fully understand Scotland and the generosity of the people that make Scotland their home.

The march just kept on going for hours. Dean, looking to grab a quick bite to eat, noticed the police starting to walk up the Royal Mile from Holyrood at 3pm, politely telling marchers to get off the road (to try to reopen the road to traffic). The remaining people trying to march to Holyrood park kept walking down the footpaths in droves! Officially, we were told the march had to end by 5pm.

Just like every other independence march, estimates of how many people attended were hard to come by. We'd heard repeated talk of well over 100,000. The fact that the march kept going for hours and never seemed to actually stop, was breathtaking. The march in Edinburgh was the longest and largest march that had ever occurred in the city. That was something for Scotland and the entire 500miles team to be proud of.

After the march wound down, the walkers had to collect their gear from Lorna's Indy van before returning home. We met up with John Robertson, our original driver, who had come to the march. We were really happy to meet up again with Evey and Mick from Auchtertyre and share our stories.

We never called for any kind of special treatment for the march, because each and everyone of the 100,000+ who attended supported our common goal - promoting an independent Scotland with our feet.

For every single marcher who attended and those who wanted to be there (and those who were there in spirit), we'd like to say just one thing:

# THANK YOU!

# BLOCKCHAIN DEMOCRACY
## 500 MILES TO BUILD A FOUNDATION

So, why was the 500 miles walk tied-in with
Blockchain Democracy? And what is Blockchain
Democracy?

Blockchain, defined in 2008, is the technology which
underpins the Bitcoin currency. Each transaction is a
'block', joined together into a 'chain'. Every block in the
chain is sequentially linked together using a validation
check that prevent fraud and tampering. The technical
term for this is a 'distributed ledger'. The most important
part to remember is that a blockchain that has been
tampered with is immediately rendered untrustworthy,
not dissimilar to a failed credit card transaction.

When applied to democracy, each block represents
a single vote and all votes from a polling area are
sequentially joined together into a chain. Using
this process in an election creates an un-hackable,
immutable, indelible ledger of voting opinions, all
available for scrutiny by inspectors such as the United
Nations.

Had this process been utilised in the 2014 referendum,
we would have had more faith in the counting process,

instead of the distrust from the results of the postal votes. Many still recall when the Scottish Conservative leader divulged results on live television, after obtaining unofficial tallies from others present for the sampling of postal votes before polling day.

Nicholas originated @YesDayScotland on Twitter in 2015. Since then he has voluntarily tracked emerging capabilities to incorporate blockchain technology into Scotland's future democracy and public services, where its use would be highly beneficial.

When the 500miles walk was conceived in May 2018, what nobody knew was that Scotland's government was about to define that they agreed with reports from YesDayScotland's investigations.

Blockchain, also referred to as 'DLT' or 'distributed ledger technology', was confirmed by the Scottish Government as the best practice for future democracy. This was defined in a report issued on July 31st, 2018 in collaboration with partner *Edinburgh's Wallet Services*.

Instead of the 500 miles walk 'campaigning' for blockchain democracy, it actually became a celebration of a brand new future for democracy in Scotland.

To help further celebrate this, YesDayScotland delivered the world's first blockchain-powered poll using a cross-platform smart phone voting application, restricting participation to 2,000 voters with a geo-location in Scotland. The project delivered flawless results, with 99.5% voting YES for Scottish independence.

On the Isle of Skye, prior to the start of the 500 miles walk, Nicholas was introduced to Ian Blackford MP,

Scotland's Westminster Leader.

Nicholas explained that he had recently delivered an article on the potential for blockchain democracy in Scotland. Martin Docherty-Hughes MP for West Dunbartonshire had been the recipient of his article. It was also published by Business for Scotland.

Ian Blackford requested that Nicholas submit best-in-world capability for Martin Docherty-Hughes, who had just recently gone on to become Scotland's Blockchain Leader in Westminster.

An overview of a pilot platform to measure desire for Scotland's independence, was defined and submitted to Martin Docherty-Hughes on the 22nd November, 2018. It was then sent to Ian Blackford and to the office of Scotland's First Minister Nicola Sturgeon, two weeks later.

All this work defined the potential of a unique global partnership between Horizon State (the 2018's World Economic Forum Technology Pioneer award winner) and a newly created blockchain identity laboratory called *BlockpassIDLab*, within Edinburgh Napier University.

Decisions were then taken, to hold the project itself as pending, so as to provide time to define what would be required to be delivered across Scotland.

On 19th February 2019, Nicholas was invited to the Scottish Parliament to meet with Mike Russell, Scotland's Cabinet Secretary for Government Business and Constitution. Here was where Nicholas delivered an overview for Scotland to receive a national scale Horizon State blockchain democracy platform. This would however, be initially dependent on the national roll-out of digital citizenship cards.

In early 2019, Nicholas was invited by Dr. Mark McNaught, Associate Professor of Law and Political Science, to incorporate distributed ledger technology into Scotland's Constitution. Dr. McNaught is a constitutional scholar and has been developing the Scottish Constitution since 2012.

In the final stages of development, the constitution project has received input from over 250 citizens from all across Scotland. This collaboration has resulted in what is now considered to be one of the world's finest written constitution's. Uniquely, it is the very first constitution to include Blockchain's distributed ledger technology. More information about this project can be found online via the website:

https://scottishconstitution.com/

Many people in Scotland don't even know what a constitution is, let alone recognise that the only countries not to have one today are New Zealand, Israel, and the individual nations that make up the UK. 'The Constitution' of each country is traditionally taught in schools worldwide.

The 500 miles walk was branded with blockchain across its span. It was the first civil rights march in history to highlight and lead the campaign for democracy underpinned with DLT. The benefits include increasing digital inclusion, voting participation, security and accountability. It also introduces reductions in environmental footprints and ultimately result in massive savings for taxpayers across public services.

An immediately noticeable benefit of DLT is access to accurate and almost instantaneous results in every election and referendum at the close of voting. Just think about not waiting into the wee hours for results.

It's worth highlighting, that the first individual to join the walk specifically to talk about Blockchain Democracy capability, was David Cox on the Isle of Skye. There were many others enquiring about it after that.

After 13 days, we were joined by Dunblane resident and Edinburgh University student, Scott Gillen. The first person under 25 to ask about Blockchain. Thank you Scott for meeting with us that day.

# MEMORIES AND FLASHBACKS
## FROM THE WALK

An old man on The Kyle of Lochalsh, pressing a fiver into someone's hand, saying 'This is what I have spare today, please take it'. The truly remarkable efforts of support driver John Robertson keeping everyone safe over the opening days. The incredible scenery, from the imposing and stunning bleakness of The Isle of Skye, to the serenity of peaceful meandering rivers. How many rivers did we cross in total, maybe someone will calculate that one! Jim Stewart revealing his actual age, and telling us he was walking for his children and grandchildren. Laura Marshall and Wren Chapman on the PA system speaking to the crowd in Aberdeen, highlighting what must be done for the future of new social justice in Scotland.

Walking mile after mile, with so many people who joined the walk. And learning - goodness we certainly all learnt. Areas, geography, local stories, history, culture. Our sincere gratitude to the many people who joined the walk, specifically with ability to walk us down quiet 'local knowledge' back roads, this was absolutely crucial to the end results.

We would never ever recommend anyone undertake a similar walk. Upon reflection, it's something of a miracle that there were no accidents. For sure, there are Highway Code rules and regulations to protect citizens who wish to walk on, or down the side of a road. In practical terms, most drivers are blissfully unaware of the legal protections for walkers. Fundamentally, if a walker is walking towards you when you are driving on the road, as is their legal right to do so, it is your responsibility to drive in a way which respects and shows safety to the walker, not the other way around.

If you are overcome by a desire to head out on a long and safe Scotland walk, a few suggestions. Nicholas recommends the stunning 117 mile Fife Coastal Path. Dean recommends hiking along the rolling Pentland Hills and around Meggethead in the Borders, both are far removed from fast moving vehicles!

To us, one of the most remarkable things about the 500 miles walk, was that it was delivered in totality without any single sit-down team discussion. Those who made up the 500 miles walker and support crew, simply applied the best available logic to the evolving challenging circumstances, and delivered. As the saying goes, teamwork is dream work. The anticipated end results were prioritised absolutely, in the interests of doing whatever is required to achieve those end results. In all honesty, we surprised ourselves at what was achieved. And the same is very much true of Scotland's circumstances. Necessary change will only be delivered via constructive action.

In moments of doubt, because there were certainly many of those…, each of us sustained the other. Everything however, was actually only made possible because of the provisions made to us, by the people of

Scotland. In a tiny way for Scotland, yet in a massive way for the walkers and project support crew, it's representative of what the future society of Scotland can become. As an independent country with our own culture and identity, we can become a kinder country, more balanced, with greater parity across the span, more kindness, more equality, more generosity to those in the most need. More inclusion, more digital inclusion. More ambition.

If a measure of any society, is best considered from the way that the most vulnerable within it are looked after, that paves the way. The 500 miles walk self-funded for the first two days, Scotland's people voluntarily stepped forward and took care of everyone for the rest of the journey. Walking the walk was only one part of it, Scotland's people helped everyone talk the talk. We were on the receiving end of unprecedented voluntary community support, repetitive collaborations from so many people, and the most amazing ongoing camaraderie. Our eternal thanks to each and everyone of you who helped.

# GATHERING THOUGHTS
## REFLECTIONS BY THE WALKERS THEMSELVES

### Dean Woodhouse

I took photographs along the way with the intention of sharing our adventures with our Yes family and also to document what we had done in this book. Nobody can say we didn't cover the miles, as we had plenty of evidence (photos and images on social media hashtagged #500miles or #500mileswalk) to prove that we most certainly had. I just wished that we could have taken better notes of names along the way!

Thanks to Martin Hannan and the team at The National, my contributions were used to get the word out about our travels. It quickly became obvious that there was no way I would make the 7pm deadline for print, since we were still walking at that point. Often I was too exhausted to use my laptop until the following morning.

I chose to walk for Scotland to prove that a free Scotland can overcome the "cringe" which is relentlessly perpetuated by the British establishment throughout their media empire.

I lived in America for over two decades and met a number of very successful Scottish immigrants. They all thrived in their own businesses once they had left the UK - success they felt they couldn't achieve beforehand. Evidence, in my mind, that an independent Scotland can accomplish so much more, once we remove the shackles to the empire.

Strangely, thanks to Brexit "the gift that keeps on giving", more and more Scots have awoken to just how damaging Westminster's influential propaganda machine really is. As a team we proved that a handful of Scots could finish the daunting task of walking 500 miles, even when all the defeatist unionists said we couldn't, joking that we wouldn't. It was no surprise that we never once made the BBC news.

It was wonderful to meet and share our hope with so many people who so obviously loved their country. We ran into a number of no supporters, and I was left wondering why they were still so very bitter about it - hadn't they won the first referendum? It was blatantly clear that the short term win was a bitter one, built on a pile of lies. Just like Brexit.

In a parallel to George Orwell's 1984 (who himself worked for the BBC - real name "Eric Blair"), I feel we are being coerced into paying for newsspeak. We unconsciously consume the heavily controlled narrative by the British Government daily. Reading the government's own McCrone Report was the reference of contradicting truth for me - making my switch from No to Yes. I realised that I couldn't continue to consume the BBC's News and current affair programmes any more, without questioning absolutely everything. I am not alone.

The British now know that the "genie is out of the bottle". Nobody goes from Yes to No, simply because once you see the contradictions to truth, it can't be un-seen. The media is their last hope for perpetuating 'normalcy'. Yet this media control directed from Westminster is slowly being eaten away, as TV licence payers choose to vote with their wallets and simultaneously cut their live TV watching habits. Many of the Yes family and younger generations have abandoned the BBC and the right-wing newspapers, removing the financing and control. The focus has now moved towards social media. The fact that news outlets regularly copy social media output as news, validating the accuracy of the medium, will not end well for them.

I'm particularly annoyed at soap operas like Eastenders, realising that these kinds of programmes are created as an addictive way to normalise the population behind a narrow-minded British monoculture. This runs in the face of Scotland's predominantly open acceptance towards everyone who calls Scotland home.

Shows like these are also meant to keep people tuned in to the BBC in order to lead them in, to watch the next carefully orchestrated newscast. It was more blatant to see living in America, observing the rise of Fox TV and the normalisation towards an angry right-wing mindset.

The mainstream media constantly defines acceptable opinions that are meant to become normalised throughout the population. Why else would people be so passionate about Brexit, not realising or caring that they are ultimately going to pay for the disastrous outcome for the rest of their lives? Why else would people in England have a hatred of Scottish politicians they have never met and would be unaffected by their work?

The BBC News reporters were at the Edinburgh march, because I watched them interviewing folk right next to me in the crowd! What they said on television did not match what happened. This was quite unsurprising to me after I'd walked the Miners Strike March in London in 1983 (age 13) and the subsequent London Poll Tax March in 1990. Both events resulted in orchestrated riots and police kettling. The crowd got the blame via carefully scripted 'news' reports. Incidents like Hillsborough and Orgreave were treated in much the same way. Corruption of truth seems to be a regular feature at the heart of news during awkward situations.

On our final day in Edinburgh, the actual numbers of marchers became meaningless as the sheer size of the record crowd was shown as huge statement to Westminster. The tide had obviously turned. People were peacefully protesting on their feet, and latecomers were getting turned away! This level of support was not going to fade away. With momentum and the constant failings of the British Government with Brexit, it could only get bigger.

I'm so proud to say my teammates and I walked for over 500 miles to the Edinburgh march all the way from the Isle of Skye. And I'm thankful we could work together to put our story to paper to record our common piece of history, and share this with everyone involved.

I hope we have offered hope to all that needed it and (re)ignited the longing to fight the good fight for all. Please get in touch if you have a story to share that involved #500Miles.  Yours aye,  Dean

## Jim Stewart

I have always sought and voted for independence since my first vote at the age of 18. Fast forward nearly 50 years and my desire for independence has not wavered. My motivation for the 500 miles walk was my Grandchildren and great-grandchildren in the hope of a better future for them when I am no longer here.

I met the 500 miler team on Skye for the first time and we quickly realised there was no forward planning other than day to day, which was the purpose of the exercise as we were relying on the good will and hospitality of Scotland's people. It then sunk in the reality of our task. The first three days were brutal, but this made the team all the more determined to finish what we started and we started gelling as a team. As word got out on social media of our journey, Scotland's peoples welcomed us into their cities, towns and villages with warm hospitality, food and accommodation. Knowing people were waiting for us each day gave us the adrenalin to keep going.

It just fills my heart the effort everyone made on our behalf and I am greetin now typing this, as this is a journey that will live with me. So many people to thank it would be unfair to name anyone in particular, but you all know who you are and I love you all. This was a journey to promote independence and inspire the Scotland's people and the wider YES movement. Personally, it was everyone in the cities, towns and villages that inspired me, and I will always feel humbled and grateful for that.

The 500 miles walkers backed up by a great support team completed their journey with an exceptional crowd in Edinburgh. Everyone we met in our journey across

234

Scotland who walked with us, cheered us on, welcomed us, fed us and put us up in their homes, followed us on social media........................... YOU are ALL #500MILE WALKERS.
  SAOR ALBA


## Cath Rolland

  I'd like to add a wee bit even though I wasn't a walker.

  I've been a nationalist/patriot since 14 yr old. Both parents were staunch labour supporters and I wasn't too aware of our country's past history. In my case independence is in my whole being & in the blood. I will do what I can, whilst I can, for Independence.


## Rick McGregor

  I remember meeting up with the 500 Mile Walkers in Dunblane, while helping out with transport logistics. Spending only a few days with them was a great experience. Sharing their stories of the walk, forged friendships that have lasted. The inspiration that they have bestowed on us is remarkable. Their dedication to complete the 500 Miles was amazing. It has spurred me on to do what I can to make sure we achieve our Independence. I consider myself to be fortunate to have met the Walkers and been part of their support. Always a joy to meet up with them on any occasion since their 500 Mile adventure and continue the friendship.

## Marlene McBay from Monifieth

I know that Scotland is a rich country whose richness is not reflected in its communities. I believe that being able to decide how our wealth is spent should be in the hands of the people who live and work in Scotland and not by anyone else whose priorities are not in Scotland.

At my age, having believed all my life in independence, I don't expect to benefit a great deal from independence but generations to come will.

## Jean Lee from Monifieth

For too long Scotland and its people have been regarded as a supply resource; whether oil, workers, land, income, soldiers etc., to be deployed to the benefit of our larger English partner whilst poverty and ill health flourish at home. The democratic deficit at Westminster means our voices and our values will always be shouted down or ignored. Time to cut loose from the British state and allow our people and land to flourish. Time to abandon the 'cringe'.

## Dave Llewellyn

What do we want?
When do we want it?
THANK YOU SCOTLAND

# ACKNOWLEDGEMENTS
## TO ALL OF SCOTLAND'S YES FAMILY

It wouldn't be fair to publish such a book without a word of thanks to our Yes family and to list off every group that helped us along our journey (in the order we met), and apologies to the other Yes groups we couldn't cover.

Yes Skye & Lochalsh
Yes Highlands & Islands
Yes Ross & Sutherland
Germans for Independence
Yes Inverness
Yes Nairn
Yes Forres
Yes Elgin
Yes Fraserburgh
Yes Peterhead
Aye Ellon
Aberdeen Independence Movement (AIM)
Yes Stonehaven Mearns
Yes Laurencekirk
Yes Brechin and Edzell (Blether~In)
Yes Forfar (Blether~In)

Yes Kirriemuir
Yes Monifieth
Keep Scotland the Brand
Yes Dundee
Yes Perth City
Perthshire Pensioners for Independence
Women For Independence - Stirling
Yes Stirling
Yes Glasgow & West
Yes Rutherglen & Cambuslang
Yes West Lothian
Yes Linlithgow
Yes 2 Kirkcaldy (Hub)
Yes Pentlands
Edinburgh Yes Hub
Yes Edinburgh & Lothians (& all Edinburgh's groups)
Yes Linton
Yes Bikers

The National newspaper
Independence Live
Pilar Fernandez & Rosalía TV
Truly Scottish TV (sadly no longer operating)
Sputnik News UK

Lyndsey Peebles
Colin Mackie (Yes Biker and driver)
Lorna Taylor
Pat Lee
Joe Grant

The backroom team who made 500 miles happen:
Cliff Serbie

Fiona Mackinnon
Mike Fenwick
"Anon"
David Cox
Neil Cameron
Andrew Stewart Murray
James Gill (who walked over 125 miles with us!)
Paul Wright

John Robertson
Kevin Bowie
The Kings Arms Hotel (in Kyleakin on Skye)


We would like to personally thank the following
  members of the SNP who took the time to meet with
  the 500 miles walkers at the following locations:

Sligachan, Isle of Skye - Ian Blackford MP
Inverness - Drew Hendry MP
Ellon - Gillian Martin MP
Brechin, Tealing and Aberlemno standing stones -
                Councillor Kenny Braes
Brechin - Councillor Bill Duff
Forfar - Councillor Lyne Devine
Dundee, Tealing and Forfar - Councillor Julie Bell
Dundee - Councillor
Breich - Councillor Pauline Clark
Kirkcaldy - Peter Grant MP
Edinburgh - Christine Grahame MSP
Edinburgh - Councillor Heather Anderson
Edinburgh - Deidre Brock MP

Cath Rolland & George Page:
Lomond Graphics & Promotions, who designed and
created hundreds of "500 Miles" badges and all the
associated 500 miles merchandise.

Tealing -thank you so much for feeding us. And a
special thanks to Jean Lee for help with fixing our feet!

To everyone at the Blether~In's in Forfar and Brechin.
Thanks again for the wonderful receptions!

Paul J Colvin "The Indy Poet" and Lorna Johnston for
your wonderful and uplifting poetry and permission to
reprint it here.

Linda Clark, thank you so much for offering to write
the foreword and help get the book to the finishing line.

Joe Cochran for donating the Volterol and a big thank
you to "Mr. Malky" and everyone else who donated
medical supplies along the way. It was very much
appreciated.

A big thank you to each and every Yes supporter and
group across Scotland who we missed (sorry!).

We have done our best to write down everything
that happened over those 500 miles, but we can
honestly say we were all much too mentally exhausted
to remember many parts of it! This book has been
an exercise in persistent teamwork to try to capture
what happened, using maps, GPS tracking records,
photographs, video conference calls, in-person

meetings and what's left of our individual memories. Please forgive us if we missed any details - especially names! Please contact us if you want to be included in a subsequent update.

If you're wondering why it took so long to publish this, we can only tell you that including everything we could took a year, waiting on publishers (only to reject us six months later) and finding numerous proofreaders was no small undertaking. A huge thanks to Laura from Yes Linton for proofreading the first half of the first working draft. I am are indebted to you for your perseverance.

Finally, to Dave Llewellyn - thank you for holding this together through thick and thin. We hit some hard times at the outset, but you came through and we worked as a wonderful team - making the impossible happen. We're all proud of you and you deserve a gold medal for getting us all over the finish line.

241

# FINANCES
## DETAILS OF CONTRIBUTIONS/EXPENSES

During the walk, Laura kept track of the contributions and payments to cover expenses.

Crowd-funding wasn't done by choice, since the organisers thought that fundraising method had been overused by the Yes movement at that point in time. Merchandise pre-sales fell through due to inadequate planning by the PR company. This meant that we had to rely on contributions as we went along.

We have condensed all the contributions and expenses we are aware of below, in order to make it easier to read than the hundreds of smaller donations.

## **Contributions**

| | |
|---|---|
| Cash contributions: | £ 584.50 |
| Contributions by Yes groups: | £ 150.00 |
| Yes Bikers: | £ 130.00 |
| Contributions by political parties (SNP): | £ 150.00 |
| **Total** | **£ 1014.50** |

# Expenses

| | |
|---|---|
| Petrol/diesel/train ticket/taxi costs: | £ 354.00 |
| Food/coffee/water: | £ 365.38 |
| Accommodation (Campsite / Hotel): | £ 135.12 |
| Medical expenses and mobile SIM card: | £ 160.00 |
| Publicity (badges / PR): | freely donated. |

We have not included items (e.g. meals and coffee) where costs were paid without our knowledge, or by the walkers themselves. No alcohol or any other unlisted products were purchased with contributions. Medical expenses covered legal over-the-counter pain relief products (such as ibuprofen tablets/gel, plasters, insoles). Some of our expenses were generously offered at a free or extremely reduced rate, and for that we are extremely grateful.

No monies were taken from any external funding source, to take time off in order to do the walk, or towards the expenses and time to produce this book.

Thanks to everyone who offered financial assistance.

We'd like to list a few of these generous contributions below: Melanie Kristopher Keel, Graeme Goodall, Paula Coy, Stonehaven SNP, everyone at Yes Peterhead, Eileen Grosset, Yes Bikers: Craig MacKenzie & Darren, and the Ashton's in Linlithgow.

We cannot thank you all enough.

Printed in Poland
by Amazon Fulfillment
Poland Sp. z o.o., Wrocław